Modern Military Spouse

The Ultimate Military Life Guide for New Spouses

By J.D. Collins, Lauren Tamm and Jo, My Gosh!

For all the military spouses and significant others looking to navigate military life. You are among friends!

Contents

Foreword
Adrianna Domingos-Lupher

There are many defining moments that shape us into the individuals we become. When my husband, then fiancé, asked me to marry him, I didn't hesitate to say yes. If we're being totally honest, I don't think I actually said yes so much as I skipped goofily around my dorm room with a big fat smile plastered across my face as my fiancé laughed at my antics. I'll just say that we understand each other. He knew what he was getting with me: a feminist, a fiercely independent woman (hold on to that one, kids), and a ride-or die-partner to the end. As a former military brat, I was pretty confident. I knew what I was getting with him as well. As the oh-so poignant cliché goes, I would follow him to the ends of the Earth. And as I now know, both God and the United States Air Force have one hell of a sense of humor.

As all good military stories start...there I was, at our first duty assignment at RAF Lakenheath, United

Kingdom. I didn't say there WE were because there was no geographic "we". The Air Force, in its infinite wisdom, moved us all the way from North Carolina to the United Kingdom to turn around and fly my husband back to the United States for eight weeks of training a week after I arrived in country. I had no job, no friends, no husband, and no GPS, but I did have a brand new license to drive on the other side of the road. First of all, can you believe they had the nerve to call me dependent? Second, being alone in a foreign country with no friends or family is scary. I can say that now. I couldn't bring myself to think about it then. Third, who has two thumbs and desperately wanted to start working on all of her professional goals? This girl right here.

Over the course his eight-week training I applied for several jobs, secured a temporary job substitute teaching, drove to London, Norwich, Cambridge, and Bury St. Edmunds, made two friends, hauled home an armoire in a Volvo Sedan and assembled it, and spent hours playing Madden 2004 training camps on our Gamecube—I was determined to whip his butt when he got home...and I did. I wiped the floor with him 60-0. Looks like somebody learned how to play defense. SAFETY!

What I didn't do was die of loneliness. I didn't sit quietly in my house. I didn't run home. I came. I saw. I put the IN in independent. I got this.

Fast-forward two more months and I had finally landed a full-time job. As part of my job training, I was required to attend the base spouse orientation. During the icebreaker, I introduced myself to the spouse next to me. As I told her how excited I was to be attending the event and that I was training to facilitate this event in the future, her eyes dimmed and with her head tilted ever so sympathetically to the side, she asked me, "How are you going to be a good military spouse if you're working?"

I don't remember anything else after that. I think I short-circuited and mentally blacked out. What I do know is that spouse's words lit a fire in my soul to encourage military spouses to live military life on their own terms.

As far as I knew, up to the time of the meeting of the Stepford Spouse, I had been a pretty kickass military spouse. I figured things out. I made things happen. I embraced adventure. And I didn't let military life keep me from achieving my dreams and vision for myself. Even though I was confident that I was on the right path for my life with my serving spouse, I couldn't find myself or my approach to military life represented in any military spouse books, articles, or guides. But I knew I wasn't alone. I couldn't be. Ultimately, the Stepford Spouse's words would serve as the fuel that motivated me to launch NextGen MilSpouse and MSB New Media which put me into orbit with amazing military spouse bloggers and writers like J.D. Collins, Lauren Tamm, and Jo, My Gosh!.

Being a military spouse during the age of social media is changing the military spouse experience, too. All of a sudden we have the ability to tap into communities for instant feedback on questions about picking the right dentist to where to go if you need a Power of Attorney. As much as I love social media for crowdsourcing about military life, I don't like my resources served side-eye and a heaping pile of judgment. In this book, you'll find none of that. Whether you have a ring (or not), or have fur babies (or human babies), or are already a seasoned spouse (we have got to find a different way to say that), this book has something to offer you or somebody you know.

When Jo, J.D., and Lauren approached me to write the foreword for *Modern Military Spouse* I couldn't have been more honored and excited. It's about time we got a guide for military spouses that offers a fresh multi-dimensional perspective of what it means to be a military spouse today. This team covers all the bases...pun totally intended. I really enjoyed reading this book and I know you will, too. It was like I was sitting down to coffee with three of the coolest military spouses I know chatting about life, lessons learned, and what it means when the one you love is serving in our nation's military.

Do you know how I know you're going to be a good military spouse? Because you're going to read this book and then pass it on to a friend.

1

Introduction

Jo

Military life is... well, if nothing else, it's different. The deployments. The trainings. The watches and the duties. The traditions. The acronyms. Good gravy, the acronyms.

It's confusing enough as it is without adding the stressors of moving, finding a new job, and ingratiating yourself with new friends... every few years. Unless you come from a military family or are a veteran yourself, chances are you've had very little experience with this whole *military thing*.

I'll be honest: I had no idea what dating—and eventually marrying— a handsome, funny, smart guy in uniform would be like. I just knew that I loved John. And I knew that I didn't want to let him go. I didn't care that he was in the military. I didn't care that I had no clue what a Permanent Change of Station (PCS) was or that I didn't know the slightest bit of military protocol. Or that I called his uniform hat a "hat" and not "a cover." (Sorry. No matter what anyone says, it's a hat.)

As our relationship developed and John popped the question, I knew I had to learn more about military life and what my future would be like. I turned to books. Over the course of a year or so, I've read more than 15 books written for military families and military spouses. With the exception of a few books, the exercise was a complete and total waste of time.

I wanted practical advice. Real stuff. I wanted to know what to expect as a military spouse. How I could cope with moving around, being far away from family, and the loss of my career. I wanted to find out how *real* people lived in such a stressful, highly mobile life. I wanted to know about the details that would make being a military spouse easier. I wanted to know how to advocate in such a bureaucratic system.

This is what I found: Reasons why a military spouse should be submissive to her husband. Books that completely left the career journey out. A suggestion that spouses have a duty to give their husbands sex... or they'll cheat during deployment.

I mean, seriously. What?

As I read, I kept shaking my head. I read some of the parts aloud to John and we laughed at them. Those books didn't speak to our life. They didn't speak to our marriage. And they certainly didn't speak to me.

I quietly carried my disdain for military self-help books until J.D. from Semi-Delicate Balance, Lauren from The Military Wife and Mom, and I decided to do something about it. J.D. and Lauren weren't too thrilled with the selection of books for military spouses either. We noticed that there aren't that many books that speak to the 21st Century, Millennial military spouse. We knew they could be better. Many of the ones available are dated now, are kind of condescending, or push a particular agenda. We don't need a book that reads like a government manual. Or one that cooks us down to being *just* spouses. Our generation of military spouses and significant others deserves a book that actually makes sense and is useful to us. That speaks to our experiences and our dreams and goals.

We care about our careers—and many of us are highly qualified in the field of our choice. We see ourselves and our partners as equals. Often, we're the ones who make financial decisions alone. We send our service members off to war and turn around to care for our kids. Some of us don't have kids. We recognize that being a military spouse has a lot of wonderful attributes...but it's not all sunshine and rainbows. Sometimes it's frustrating. Sometimes it's devastatingly hard.

So we decided to write a book. After all, who better to write about being military spouses than military spouses? We want this to be a conversation between friends at a coffee shop over cookies and coffee or a discussion on a living room couch with a glass of wine in our hands.

Because it's a discussion, you'll hear the three of our voices throughout the book. We've each written different chapters that play to our strengths and our experiences as military significant others and then spouses. You'll see our names at the beginning of each chapter so you know who's talking.

About Us

J.D., Lauren, and I met like many military spouses do now: online. We each blog about military life and over time, we've struck up a friendship. We'll share more about ourselves throughout the book— so you can get to know us better— but here are our quick introductions:

- J.D. is the youngest among the three of us and blogs at Semi-Delicate Balance. She covers mostly military topics and is known for her humorous listicles that detail the funnier, more ridiculous side of military life.

- Lauren splits her blog between the military life and the mom life on her site, The Military Wife and Mom. She's a huge fan of helping parents hack parenthood through methods that she's tried with her children.

- I'm Jo and I write at Jo, My Gosh! where I share mostly military-related posts with a side of care package and blogging advice. My husband and I currently don't have any kids.

We're so glad that you're starting this conversation with us and we're thrilled to help you get through some of the bumps and obstacles of being a military spouse. It's pretty spectacular that you're along for the ride. Thanks for trusting us. Now, let's get started.

2

When You Don't Have a Ring

J.D.

I was a Navy significant other for exactly three years and six months. That's considered a lifetime in the military world. I moved 3,000 miles to be with him. I had to re-strategize my career path as well as family planning. I've had to miss celebrations for family and friends. I spent months worrying and stressing over the safety of his life during deployments and separations. I did all this...*without a ring*.

It was like having one foot in and one foot out of the military world. And I know how that feels. Without a dependent ID card, it may seem like you "don't count." Let me tell you something: you *do* count. Just because you don't receive base access or military insurance doesn't mean that you don't go through the same hurt and pain as a military spouse does during the tribulations of military life.

Do the following statements sound familiar?

- Waiting for your service member to pick you up to get on base.

- Stressing over deployments knowing you wouldn't be called because you're not next of kin.

- Handing over cash to your service member at the Commissary because, heaven forbid, you pay the cashier directly.

- Trying not to judge or compare the other military couple who married after one week of dating.

- Awkward silence when correcting people when they called you a spouse.

- Getting "the look" when you said you and your partner are "only dating right now."

- Hearing "I couldn't do that," "I would never," or "You must be crazy."

- Feeling like the most important person in the eyes of your service member... but not the eyes of anyone else.

Being branded as "just the significant other" doesn't feel good, but you know what does feel good? Being in love.

Love, trust, communication, and mutual respect—those things will help carry you along in your relationship. Military life is an obstacle, but it offers the perspective you need to determine if military life is for you. Those obstacles strengthen your relationship more than ever.

If you discover military life isn't for you, don't sweat it. Not every relationship is meant to be. Learn from it and move on.

If military life is for you, and your relationship is destined to last, then military life is the ultimate test that can strengthen your relationship for the long run.

Tips for Dealing with Naysayers

If you experience negativity in the military community while filling the role of military significant other, there are several ways you can turn the situation into a positive encounter.

Change the Subject

It may feel uncomfortable talking about the status of your relationship when you're unsure yourself. Since you can't predict the future, perhaps change the topic. Divert it to something else that is happening with your relationship: buying new furniture, going on a trip, your last date night, your next anniversary. Better yet, you can ask other people how their relationship is going. They don't seem to mind prying into yours, perhaps give them a polite taste of their own medicine.

Kill Them with Kindness

Smile, nod, and address the negativity with positivity. For example, I would respond to a naysayer, "No, we're not married yet, but we are very happy in our relationship. Thank you for asking." When a naysayer would suggest that you must be crazy, respond with something fun or off the cuff such as "Just crazy in love." When a naysayer would say that they "could never do that" or they "don't understand how you deal with it", respond, "It's not for all, but it works for us. I don't expect you to understand, but I would greatly appreciate your support."

Ignore It

If all else fails and the naysayers are still criticizing your relationship, ignore it. The type of person who judges without knowing your relationship is not the type of person you need in your life. Simply say,

"That's kind of personal for me to talk about," politely excuse yourself, and walk away.

Resources for the Military Significant Other

As a military significant other, you may feel many resources are unavailable to you. However, there also may be resources available that make an effort to include military significant others.

FRG

The Family Readiness Group (FRG) varies from command to command. Some are very welcoming and inclusive of significant others. Some... well, not so much. Contact the command FRG leader and find out if significant others are included on important command information. More often than not, especially during deployment, FRG groups welcome any and all family or friend contact for service members. If they're not super inclusive, you can still offer to volunteer. That way, you may be able to get in their good graces.

Social Media Groups

Some local spouse support groups welcome significant others, some don't. Don't take it personally. It may feel like some exclusive club, but it's really not. With some internet research and online forums, you can also find support that way. There are many different significant other groups as well. A couple of words of caution about social media groups, as we live in a different era now. Remember to keep OPSEC and PERSEC in mind when discussing your personal life and the military life. This goes for questions, posts, and pictures (see Chapter 13). Also, remember that the internet makes everyone think they have a right to say whatever they please. This may involve harsh or rude comments and can lead to drama. Avoid participating in negative conversations online, as that is the last thing you would need.

Other Significant Others

The best way to gain support as a military significant other is to seek out other significant others. Ask your service member if he or she knows any more military significant others for you to network among; then host a get-together to meet each other. Don't be afraid to socialize with military spouses. They were also significant others themselves at one point and can serve as a great resource after experiencing many of military life's ups and downs. Some are more than willing to help others but you won't know until you ask.

Ring or no ring, you are an important part of your service member's life. You chose your partner and with your partner comes this crazy military journey. There will be ups and downs, but remember the best part: You're in this together.

3

When Your Service Member's Gone

Jo

I am a crier.

Oh boy, am I a crier. When John left for Afghanistan, I was a sloppy, weepy mess. I cried before he left. I cried while saying goodbye. I cried after he left... for four hours... as I drove through two states.

And the next day, I cried too.

Once I (finally) stopped crying, I realized that there was a very, very, very long time between that goodbye and the next hello. It was bone-crushingly awful to think about. I knew I had to deal with it constructively. I couldn't cry forever.

Separations are part of military life. They're something we know will happen, even if we're not sure when they will happen. Between boot camp, TAD/TDYs, deployment, geobaching, and other reasons, chances are, if you haven't experienced saying goodbye to your main squeeze already, you will soon.

No matter how many times you say goodbye, most military spouses will agree that it doesn't get easier. You will still miss your partner. You'll still dread the goodbye. You'll still wait on pins and needles for his or her return.

But in the meantime, you'll have to cope with whatever time you'll be apart. It's tough, but you can do it. I promise.

Feel All the Feels

If you're looking for the classic "Suck it up, buttercup" speech, you won't find it here. I'm not going to tell you to put on your "Big Girl Panties" either. It's okay to be sad. It's okay to be angry at the military. It's okay to be frustrated or worried or to feel any of the millions of other feelings that come with a separation. Those feelings are valid. They change with time and they change with the kind of separation you're experiencing.

Own your feelings. Deal with them. If that means you need to go sit in a closet and listen to Yanni, do it. If it means you need to talk to your pastor, do it. If it means you need to have a good cry on the phone to your mom, do it.

Reach Out to Your Circle

Often, I think military spouses believe they have to embody the same kind of machismo that oozes from the military. Not true. You don't have to sport a stiff upper lip when you feel like you're dying inside. You don't have to go it alone. Reach out to the people who you trust and who support you. Tell them what you need and how you feel. Ask them for help.

Get Help if You Need It

A large percentage of military spouses deal with anxiety and depression. We often don't get help ourselves because we're taking care of others or we feel embarrassed. Some spouses, sadly, have even attempted or completed suicide. If you feel hopeless, there are people and organizations who can help support you (see Chapter 15).

Make a List

When John was deployed, I made a list of 100 things I wanted to do in the year he was gone. They ranged from books I wanted to read to crafts I wanted to try to completing different races (even though I'm not a runner). I was working full-time, but this list helped me think constructively about the weekends that we otherwise would have shared together. It helped me focus on more than just myself. And it helped me do some really cool things (like start my blog)!

Keep On Keepin' On

Once you're done throwing yourself on the bed all Scarlett-O'Hara-style, it's time to pick yourself up, dust yourself off, and get back to doing your thing. You're someone with things to do and places to go. You can't (and shouldn't) sit around staring at the walls waiting for his or her return. After all, you're only this age once. This is the youngest you'll ever be again in your life—so make it count. Go to work. Keep to your routine. Go out with friends.

Step Away from the Cell Phone

Really. It's okay if you're away from your cell phone to go for a run or take a bubble bath. It's okay not to be connected all the time. And anyway, being constantly connected to your phone can make the time apart feel even longer, more tedious, and more depressing.

Be Positive

Surround yourself with people who are positive thinkers. Find quotes, song lyrics, or verses that speak to you and make you feel empowered, calm, and strong. Treat your body and mind kindly and cut yourself a break. You can't be Super Woman or Super Man all the time.

Find a Rhythm That Works for You

Your schedule might be different during a separation than it is when your partner is home. Embrace your new routine. Find joy in the things that you're able to do at this moment, rather than always thinking about what's missing.

Sleep, for Goodness' Sake

I say this with all of the love in my heart: sleep, you crazy night owl. I was the worst offender of this rule during John's deployment. But guess what? Staying up to all hours of the night, hoping for a 30-second Google chat conversation will not make tomorrow feel better. And over time, it will run you down, make you sick, and make you sad. Ultimately, it will make the separation much, much harder than it has to be.

Foster Your Relationship

Whether it's through handwritten cards, good morning text messages, or another way that you find connection and communication with your partner, fostering your relationship and growing it into something stronger and even more beautiful than when he or she left is a really satisfying and wonderful thing to do. There's no limit to how you can do this, just like there's no right or wrong way.

Ready for the next separation? It's okay if you're not. But having the tools to cope and deal with it when it comes is important. You've got this.

4

Preparing for a Successful Military Marriage

Jo

Marriage is awesome.

If you find the right person who makes your heart sing, who supports you, who you're happy to see (mostly) every day, it is the best thing in the entire world. No hyperbole. That's a fact. And although we all have different obstacles in our lives because of our partner's military service, it is possible to create the foundation for a successful military marriage if both parties want to put in the work. And when I say work, I really don't mean work. It's a pure joy.

Spirit of Possibility

The military throws a lot of stuff our way and it's frustrating. I get it. I know. Been there, done that, got the butt-depression on the couch and empty bags of chips to prove it. But sweet goodness, if you can't be a little positive about the situation you're in, it will take a toll on your relationship.

Believe me, I'm not just talking about you. So often, I receive emails from readers who are frustrated because their partners tell them that the relationship is on the spouse. They have to be sexier. They have to do more while the other is on deployment. They have to be available at every beck and call when he or she gets home.

And there's no reciprocation.

I don't believe in settling debts in your marriage (we'll get to that in a minute), but believe me—a relationship without a spirit of possibility is one that is in serious trouble. If your spouse isn't going to pitch in and help to nurture your relationship, it's going to be a lot harder than it has to be.

So practice a spirit of possibility in your marriage. Often, readers ask me what they can do for their partner—especially during deployment or long separations. I respond with suggestions, and often, the person I'm corresponding with will shoot every suggestion down. Email him? Nope. He doesn't check his email. Write a letter? Nope—it takes too long. Send a care package? I don't know what to send. Skype with her? Not worth it—the resolution is so bad, I can't see her face. I totally understand that everyone has different circumstances—especially those with partners serving in really tough places (like miles below the surface of the ocean)—but come on. Where there's a will there's a way! You can foster your relationship even though the military makes it a little rougher than what it could be. Get some pluck!

Instead of just saying no and dismissing ideas, what can you say yes to? What can you do to make your partner feel more loved, more respected, or more cared for in the situation you're in? And talk to your partner about the same thing. What can he or she do to make life easier for you? How can your partner show you he or she cares, respects, and loves you even from thousands of miles away?

Settling Debts

Before I got married, my mom gave me a note that said something like, "Marriage isn't about 50-50. It's about 100-100." At another time, someone wisely told me that some days, your marriage will be 20-80. Other days it will be 100-0. Some days it will be 50-50.

Lots of numbers. And it seems like the percentages all contradict themselves. But hear me out. The ideas both have the same point: if you each keep a mental score card of all of the things you do and don't do, you're going to live a very bitter life. You can't build a generous marriage when you're thinking about how you're going to get yours or how you need to repay your spouse for something he or she did yesterday.

And what's the fun in that anyway?

I love surprising John and doing nice things for him—not because I want to be repaid in some way (although brownies are always nice)—but because I love seeing his face light up. I love making him happy and making his life easier. I love letting him know that I think about him constantly and that I am willing to take the time and effort to put those thoughts to action.

In a military marriage, it is really easy to let the debts pile up. It's easy to feel like the victim in a life where you don't make decisions, where you have no agency. Instead, think of the two of you as a unit. It'll make it easier to see that PCS to Nowheresville, USA as something that the both of you did together, rather than something you did for your partner. Or that tough deployment as something you both accomplished (albeit in different ways), rather than something you were dragged through. After all, that's the point of marriage, being a unit with another person and tackling life together.

Communication

I could write an entire book on communication in relationships, but I only have a few paragraphs to talk about this massively important subject. In our marriage, we don't go to bed angry. We tried doing it once. It ended up in a fight the next day that was the biggest of our entire relationship because we let it fester. It was horrible. And we decided that never, ever again would we treat our relationship that way.

Even though I'm a little on the quiet side (hey, I'm a writer, what did you expect?), we have both committed to communicating with each other no matter what. Even when it's tough. Even when we don't want to talk. Even when we're tired.

It'll be awkward at first, but keep going, even when you feel dumb. Openly communicating with each other leads to a more fulfilling and happier relationship. It is incredibly rewarding. You know where your partner stands. He or she knows where you stand. You both feel listened to, validated, and valuable. You're able to talk about issues before they become big deals rather than icing each other out or getting into a screaming match when the issue blows up.

Honesty and Trust

Every relationship needs honesty and trust to be able to function. And perhaps military relationships need it just a little bit more.

Being committed to being honest and truthful in your marriage is a direct outgrowth of your marriage vows. It's the bedrock of your relationship—the thing on which you build everything else. Being dishonest or untrustworthy is the easiest way to create a rift in your marriage. When it comes down to it, if you and your partner respect each other and respect your marriage, if you treasure it, you will do everything in your power to be honest and trustworthy regardless of the situation you're in. (And so will your partner! It's not a one-way street.)

There are some awful stereotypes in the military community about cheating. Military spouses who put brooms on their porches when their husbands are away to signal that they're available. Officers who woo junior enlisted members on deployment. Couples who have agreements about cheating during deployment and separations. Female service members who try to steal away their male coworkers.

33

Those stereotypes lead people to believe that infidelity is the norm in military relationships that it's just what everyone does. It's pretty insulting, actually.

Infidelity exists in the military. There's no doubt about that. But it isn't inevitable and it's no reason to cold shoulder the women at your husband's command. It's no reason to be glaringly suspicious of your husband when he hasn't contacted you the first day of his deployment. It's no reason to think that you can't trust your partner just because he or she is in the military.

Legal Documents

Oh, bureaucracy. If you're just marrying into the military, get ready for a lot of red tape, lines, waiting, and awkward websites that don't work quite right. It will be a learning process. Take a deep breath, grab a binder, and start gathering documents.

Marriage Certificate

One of the most important documents you can possibly have is your marriage certificate. This sounds stupid, but make sure that it's a legal document. Some states actually issue decorative, display copies of marriage licenses... which aren't legal. The military will not accept them.

How do I know this? Because John and I only had a decorative certificate when I tried to enroll for military benefits and an ID. It was the only one we were presented with at our wedding and thought that it *was* a legal document. We didn't know that there were two different kinds and it caused huge headaches. The military absolutely would not accept our certificate as it was, and we had to send away and wait for the legal copy of the certificate before I could become recognized as a military spouse.

When you register for your license, double-check and ask the clerk if you'll be receiving a legal copy of the certificate. If not, insist that you do. Some states will waive the fee for military couples.

Birth Certificate

Make sure that you have your birth certificate and copies of it. Get it out of your parents' safe and put it into yours.

Photo ID

Keep a copy of your driver's license—even if you're not driving where you're stationed. Having another form of ID with your name on it is really very useful and may be necessary to have some documents issued to you. You will also want to have a passport issued in your legal name so that you are able to travel at a moment's notice—which is especially important if your service member is hurt overseas and you need to get to him quickly.

ID Card

To get onto base and to receive benefits that you're entitled to, you'll need a military ID card. Check with the on-base ID card office for what kinds of information and documentation you'll be required to bring along.

Social Security Card

Yep, get this out of your parents' safe, too.

Other things to do:

- Get enrolled into the Defense Enrollment Eligibility Reporting System (DEERS).

- Become the general and durable Power of Attorney for your spouse, especially if he or she will be leaving on deployment, TAD/TDY, geobaching, or going to bootcamp.

- Create a will; if you have children, make sure to incorporate guardianship for them, too.

- Register your vehicle with the base—if you need to. Some bases no longer require vehicle registration; others do. Find out what your bases' stipulations are.

- Become a life insurance beneficiary.

- Register for TRICARE (the military insurance provider) health care benefits.

- Register for dental health care benefits.

Legal Information for Spouses

When you marry your spouse, you're getting into a (sometimes confusing) system that has some of its own rules and regulations. As a military spouse, just as you have benefits from marrying your service member, you also have legal rights. There are many nuances to those rights, so I won't enumerate them here. But you can check them out on your own:

- Military OneSource Legal Information (http://www.militaryonesource.mil/financial-and-legal)

- Military.com Free Legal Assistance (http://www.military.com/benefits/military-legal-matters/legal-assistance-and-jag/free-legal-assistance.html)

- American Bar Association Military Legal Assistance and Civil Matters

(http://www.americanbar.org/portals/public_reso
urces/aba_home_front/information_center/worki
ng_with_lawyer/information_about_lawyers/milit
ary_legal_assistance/civil_matters.html)

You deserve to be in a healthy relationship free of fear
and abuse. If you think you may need help, there are
resources to support you:

- Military OneSource Child Abuse and Domestic
  Abuse (http://www.militaryonesource.mil/abuse)

- Military OneSource Domestic Abuse Military
  Reporting Options
  (http://www.militaryonesource.mil/abuse?conten
  t_id=266707)

- How to Help Service-Connected Victims of
  Domestic Abuse
  (http://www.militaryonesource.mil/abuse?conten
  t_id=266711)

- Real Warriors Domestic Violence Resources for
  Military Families
  (http://www.realwarriors.net/family/support/dom
  esticviolence.php)

When it comes down to it, a military relationship is
just the same as any other relationship under the sun.
It takes time, commitment, energy, love, trust, and
respect. As in any other relationship, there are

obstacles you must figure out together. Some of them are because of the military. Others are not. And yes, it sometimes feels easier to blame the military or your circumstances for rough patches or frustrations. Don't give into the temptation. When it comes down to it, your relationship is yours and your partner's. Protect it. Guard it. And nourish it.

5

Creating a Budget that Works

Lauren

Before I even met my husband, I was all too familiar with the strain finances can put on even the healthiest of marriages. It's easy to see how financial infidelity or even simple disagreements can cause discord within a family. All you have to do is turn on the TV to see couples divorcing left and right fighting over money and other nanny-boo-boo nonsense.

Knowing that little pearl of information, it became my mission to ensure finances would never cause major stress or sabotage a relationship. Of course that doesn't mean money never causes any stress in our life. But there are *so many* awesome things you can do to financially-proof your life and make things a whole lot easier on your marriage and family.

Military marriages are challenging and the last thing you need is to worry about scraping your pennies together to pay the bills. Once my husband and I were engaged to be married and several years into married life, there are several things that we do to keep our financial house in order:

Set Financial Goals with Your Spouse

Before we were married, my husband and I were both pretty darn comfortable spending our money the way we wanted. During our pre-marital counseling, we created financial goals for our future together.

What do you really want your financial house to look like in 5, 10, 20, and 30 years? And if you want it to look like XYZ, how are you going to reach those goals? It's one thing to want a log cabin in the Rocky Mountains and another thing to actually develop a step-by-step plan to achieve that goal.

Embrace Transparency

If you read this chapter and take only one thing away, let it be this: financial transparency is the key to a successful marriage. You and your service member should both know exactly how much money each of you earns, spends and saves. You should both look at bank, credit card, and investment statements together each month. And you absolutely must know how much debt you both carry and actively plan to pay it off.

As a married couple, you are far more likely to succeed in budgeting when you are accountable to each other and building financial trust in your relationship. This doesn't mean you can't have fun and buy special things. It means that you don't keep financial secrets from each other. It means that you don't secretly establish a credit card without your spouse knowing and purchase items and hide them each month.

For my husband and I, establishing transparency eliminated fights over finances. Now we focus more on fighting over other things like putting the toilet seat down or what TV show to watch.

Pay Down Debts

If you have debt, it's important to develop a plan to pay it off. Set priorities by listing which debt you need to pay off first. Many financial advisors recommend paying off the debt with the highest interest rate first, while paying what's required on your remaining debts. Then move onto each subsequent debt until they all are gone.

If you are struggling with high interest rates, you can lower your credit card interest rates by doing a balance transfer. This means that when you move your credit card to another bank, they will lower the interest rate to get your business. Shop around and try to get the lowest interest rate for the longest duration (preferably until it's paid off completely).

Live Off One Income

One thing that we started doing before we were even married was to pretend my income didn't *even exist*. All of it went straight to savings for various financial goals. We budgeted down to the penny using only his income.

This is for two reasons:

- Military spouse employment can be a bumpy road. Treating your income as savings can save you stress when unemployment hits.

- It helps you reach greater financial goals in a shorter period of time when you are saving an entire income.

Pay Off All of Your Bills on Time

You are probably nodding yes, already knowing that this is common information. But I can't tell you how many people I know who are racking up credit card debt, late fees, and other unnecessary bills.

Paying your bills on time, and if you choose to use credit cards, always paying off the balance **in-full each month** will save you thousands, if not more, in the long run. As a rule of thumb, never spend more than you can pay off. USAA and Navy Federal both offer a cash back credit card, which allows you to earn a percentage back on every purchase you make.

Create a Monthly Budget

Together we created a spreadsheet and itemized all of our necessary expenses, as well as incidental expenses. You can download our free excel spreadsheet to Google docs for yourself to use: http://www.themilitarywifeandmom.com/modern-military-spouse-printables/. Password: MILITARY20

Using a budget, set financial priorities. Examine what you really need to spend each month and what can you minimize or live without. Evaluating priorities and seeing how monthly income breaks down month after month can work wonders when it comes to sticking to a financial plan.

The kicker? When my husband saw how much our savings was growing each month on the spreadsheet, it helped him become *even more committed* to our future financial goals.

Hold Monthly Budget Meetings

Financial transparency is huge, huge, huge. One way to regularly maintain transparency is to hold a monthly financial meeting. In our home, it usually takes less than one hour per month to review everything together. Did you stick to the budget? Where did you fall short? Be open and honest with each other. Monthly meetings will help you stay on track and make adjustments with the budget.

Have a Monthly Cash Spending Allowance

One major way to cut back on spending is simply to have a "no questions asked" monthly cash allowance. My husband and I each get $100 in cash every month. We both use the money to buy unnecessary things that we really want: lunch out with a friend, a pedicure, a new pair of shoes *when I already had 15*, a special item off Amazon, etc. You make the rules for the cash allowance, but it's an awesome way to still feel like you have freedom to spend some money without going overboard.

Create an Emergency Fund

Creating an emergency fund is the cornerstone of financially-proofing your life. When things come up you will easily be able to pay for it using your emergency fund. **It's recommended to keep approximately 6 months' worth of living expenses in your emergency fund.**

Sounds like a lot of money! And it is! But that is what will really save you when the car breaks down, you lose your job, the house incurs major damage, etc.

Invest in a Roth Individual Retirement Arrangement (IRA) for Both Spouses

It's easy *not* thinking about how you will live month to month once you are both retired. You might count on a military pension to support you and your partner in the future, but it's far from a guarantee. On top of that, it's definitely not a guarantee that the pension will be enough to support you both through retirement.

Investing in a Roth IRA is the most tax efficient way to privately save for retirement. Most military families expect to be in the same or higher tax bracket when they retire, which is why the Roth IRA is a great option. It allows you to pay taxes on the money now rather than later. This means all investment earnings are tax-free since you are not taxed during future retirement withdrawals as long as you meet certain IRS requirements.

If you are interested in creating a Roth IRA or investing in a retirement account, here are 3 great places to start:

- Vanguard.com

- USAA.com

- TSP.gov

Thrift Savings Plan (TSP), Vanguard, and USAA will allow you to easily set up target date retirement funds, make investing extremely inexpensive and incredibly simple for even the most amateur investor.

If you are interested in setting up a retirement account through TSP, you have two options:

- Traditional (pre-tax): You defer paying taxes on your contributions and their earnings until you withdraw them. If you are a uniformed services member making tax-exempt contributions, your contributions will be tax-free at withdrawal but your earnings will be subject to taxation.

- Roth (after-tax): You pay taxes on your contributions as you make them (unless you are making tax-exempt contributions), and your earnings are tax-free at withdrawal as long as you meet certain IRS requirements.

A great resource to learn more about retirement planning is Military Financial Planner (http://militaryfinancialplanner.com/).

Invest in a College 529 Plan for the Kids

Did you know that in 20 years it will cost a college-bound student approximately $250,000 to complete a 4-year degree at a public university? That is insane! Even if you only wanted to contribute 20% to *one* child's college education, that would be $50,000.

You can choose a state 529 college investment plan for any state that you want—even if you don't live there! There are a few states that have their 529 plans really nicely put together.

Here are the top five in the nation according to *Forbes* magazine:

- Maryland College Investment (http://www.collegesavingsmd.org/college-investment-plan-overview.aspx)

- Arkansas T. Rowe Price College (http://individual.troweprice.com/public/Retail/Products-&-Services/College-Savings-Plans)

- Nevada Vanguard 529 (https://investor.vanguard.com/529-plan/vanguard-529-plan)

- Utah Educational Savings (http://www.uesp.org/)

- Ohio College Advantage 529 (http://www.collegeadvantage.com/home)

You don't receive a state tax deduction if you don't live or file taxes in that state. However, many military families move frequently and will file taxes in various states over the years. Before you consider any of these plans, take a look at your state's offering. They may offer a tax break for residents that could make it worth your while if you plan to file taxes in a given state for some time. If you want to rollover your 529 plan to another state, it is possible, but there are significant rules and tax laws to follow in order to properly complete a rollover. My best advice? Choose a state plan wisely and save yourself the trouble of a 529 rollover.

Another important benefit of the many 529 plans is that other family members can make a donation to the college fund with just a few simple clicks. Also, if one child does not go to college, you can roll it over to another child.

Utilize Discounts, Freebies and Coupons When You Can

Again obvious, but true. If a military discount is offered, don't be afraid to politely take it. Here are a few online resources to help find discounts specific to military families:

- Military Shoppers (https://militaryshoppers.com/)

- Thrifty Shopaholic (http://thriftyshopaholic.com/)

- Budget Loving Military Wife (http://www.budgetlovingmilitarywife.com/)

- Retail Salute (http://www.retailsalute.com/)

- Army Wife 101 Military Discounts (http://armywife101.com/category/military-life-2/freebies-and-discounts)

- Singing Through the Rain Military Discounts (http://www.singingthroughtherain.net/2011/02/military-discounts-2.html)

Minimize, Downsize, and Keep It That Way

The *best* way to save money is simply *not to spend it* in the first place. Opting to live in a smaller home, accumulating less stuff, and forgetting about keeping up with the Joneses will save you tens of thousands in the long run, and it will help secure your strong financial future.

Regardless of income, budgets are feasible for all families. Learn what you can and cannot afford, stick to a monthly budget, choose wise investments for both college 529 plans and retirement accounts, and build trust through financial transparency. Years down the road, when finances are a breeze, paying bills is stress-free, and your military marriage is healthy, you will be so glad you took a few small steps to create lifelong financial freedom.

6

Hitting the Books Military-Style

Jo

If you've never gone through the college search before, it can be daunting. (And exciting too!) Add in a PCS or deployment, and it can be downright tough. As an instructor for a graduate program, I've seen the importance of choosing the school that's right for you first-hand. It doesn't matter if you want to earn your associate's, bachelor's, master's, or Ph.D—only you know your particular situation and abilities and what is best for you and your family.

Be Honest

Be honest with yourself on the college search. Be honest about your passions, interests, and skills and what you see yourself doing in the future. Be honest about your family's financial situation. Be honest about how you learn and what kind of school setting you see yourself in. Once you're able to have a frank discussion with yourself about your goals and dreams, you'll be able to more clearly look for schools that fit your unique needs.

Know the Fine Print

From the 9/11 GI Bill to MyCAA, many military families just don't know all of the benefits that are available to them. Create a binder for the college search and compile all of your known benefits. Read the fine print. Know what terms your benefits are on and what kinds of schools accept them. Ask questions and get solid answers.

Often, military families only look to the military for help financing their education. But seriously, leave no stone unturned. If you're employed by an organization that offers scholarships or educational funds, check that out.

Post-9/11 GI Bill

The Post-9/11 GI Bill is an education benefit for veterans who served after September 10, 2001 and had at least 90 days of continuous service (including

Reserve and Guard members) are eligible. While there are many specific details and stipulations, the basic benefits are these:

- tuition and school fees

- living stipend

- allowance for books and supplies

The educational benefit you receive also depends on the length of the military member's service and possible disability (if the member had a medical discharge). Make sure that you read the fine print and know what applies to your unique situation.

The Post-9/11 GI Bill also offers the Yellow Ribbon Program, a list of schools (both public and private) that offer additional funding in conjunction with Veterans Affairs to help cover costs that the GI Bill may not cover at their particular institution. If your dream school seems a little out of reach financially, make sure you inquire if they're part of the Yellow Ribbon Program or check out this list of participating schools here: http://www.benefits.va.gov/gibill/yellow_ribbon.asp.

Finally, the GI Bill does offer service members the opportunity to share their benefits with family members. The ability to transfer the Bill to dependents comes with a caveat: an additional amount of service time may be added to his or her contract. The GI Bill can be transferred in part or whole to spouses and children.

MyCAA

MyCAA stands for My Career Advancement Account, a governmental program provided by the Department of Defense that helps to pay for workforce development educational opportunities exclusively for military spouses. MyCAA pays $4,000 total (with a cap of $2,000 per year). Depending on your chosen field, the scholarship may help you pursue and complete a license, certificate, certification, or associate degrees. It can even help you complete graduate credits.

The basic idea is to give spouses the ability to build a portable career through this program, so there are stipulations both on the types of programs you can enter and the spouses who are able to use the program— including branches (Coast Guard spouses are not eligible) and your spouse's rank.

Other possibilities for funding include:

- employer tuition assistance programs

- private scholarships

- federal loans and grants

- private loans and grants

- scholarships and grants offered by schools

Know Your Responsibilities

For many military spouses, going to college full-time is not an option. Even if you're technically taking the credits that make you a full-time student, you probably have other responsibilities that take time away from your studies. Think about it—the kids, the pet, a job, not to mention battening down the hatches during a deployment or keeping everything running smoothly during your partner's watch schedules. There's a lot to handle.

As an online graduate school instructor, I've seen students leave the program I teach at because they simply hadn't inventoried their responsibilities ahead of time. Often they end up having to deal with the financial ramifications of leaving the program, too. Make no mistake: it is tough to juggle your academics, family, and career. Keep this in mind as you create your educational plan. Realistically, will you finish your bachelor's degree in four years? What about the overseas PCS happening in a year? Will you be able to go to school part-time or full-time?

The answers to these questions may also impact the funding you can receive. Remember too, that you may be required to pay back a portion or all of certain types of funding if you fail a class or leave a program before finishing it. That's why being realistic and really thinking about your capacity as a caregiver, student, and employee is important right off the bat.

Know Yourself

If you only knew how many times I receive frustrated or panicked emails and phone calls from my grad students who tell me they aren't online learners. Often these students aren't doing well in class or they expected online learning to be less difficult, less rigorous, or less time-consuming than an in-person class. At that point, it truly is too late for me to help them. If they don't have the technological skills or the interest in taking an online class, there is really nothing I can do except encourage them and give them pointers on how to cope with learning online. This is all to say: know who you are and what your abilities are. Know what kinds of learning you enjoy and at which you excel. And then look for programs and schools that can enhance your skills and help you learn the way you do best.

Look for Support

To put it very unscientifically, there are a ton of military-connected students in college today. With the

GI Bill and force drawdowns, many veterans are in the college classroom (and many of their spouses can finally go back to school now that they are settled down). Because the veteran population increased in higher education rather drastically over the last ten years or so, many schools now offer help to military-affiliated learners. Make sure you ask about support systems (which may include clubs, counselors, or a student affairs department) put in place for military spouses. Hey— it can't hurt to ask!

Types of Programs

Online

Online learning is much different than learning in person, and it is possible to get an excellent education from an online program. While it gives you unprecedented freedom in your schedule and where you can learn, it also can be tough if you're not someone who can buckle down and teach themselves the material or can organize time to study every day. Online classes are often more work-intensive than traditional classes. You will have to be a go-getter who reads a ton—from class announcements to discussion board posts to the textbook. You'll need to set aside time to learn and to work because you won't have a schedule telling you what time to be in class. You'll need to be proactive about contacting your professors because you won't see them every week.

If you know you'll be moving a lot, you might want to heavily consider online education since you can take your school with you and won't have to go through the headache of transferring schools or credits every time you PCS. You'll also be able to stay on your graduation/completion time table, which could mean less money spent and less time wasted waiting for transfers to go through.

Traditional

When you think of college, these are the kinds of programs you think of: a professor lecturing at the front of the room, you busily taking notes in auditorium-style seating. Going to a brick-and-mortar school is much harder to do as a military spouse if you're planning on moving with your spouse. However, some bachelor's and master's degree programs cannot be done online or you may feel that you'll miss out if you don't have the experience of walking across the quad on your way to class. There are military spouses out there who earned their degrees while their spouses served in other states or other countries. If you want to earn your degree from a traditional college, figure out how you'll do the military thing. Will you PCS and transfer your credits and school? (If you do, remember that transferring credits is often difficult. Many times they will not transfer 100% which could add both time and financial burden to your schooling.) Will you stay put for years? Will you do it after your spouse leaves the military?

Community College

Sometimes going by the names "two-year college" or "junior college," community colleges are much more localized and offer different kinds of programs for different kinds of learners. For whatever reason, community colleges get a bad rap, but they're actually a great place to get more focused, individualized attention from professors, cheaper tuition rates, and flexible scheduling. Because most community college students don't go to school full-time, you'll find a lot of night and weekend classes. Most community college programs provide pathways to help you earn your associate's or bachelor's degree, certification, technical training, or non-degree skills. Most likely, you will need to transfer your credits to a four-year college to finish your bachelor's (check with your counselor so you're absolutely sure), but you'll most likely end up with a cheaper overall price tag on your education.

Technical Programs

Most technical schools are two-year institutions that focus on job-ready skills like plumbing or culinary art. Technical programs can be public, private, or for-profit— with many of the highly publicized ones being for-profit schools. And while we're on the subject, let's talk about private, public, and for-profit schools.

Private

Private non-profit institutions, sometimes called independent, often run by religious institutions, are simply ones that can set their own policies and goals because they are not beholden to federal and state funds. Private schools are funded by donors and are usually known for having a higher price tag than public institutions. However, private schools often make concerted efforts to offer scholarships and grants to many of students, so the cost of a private school may be considerably cheaper once you speak to a counselor or financial aid officer.

Public

Public non-profit colleges and universities are usually founded by the government (state or federal) with the purpose of creating opportunities for affordable higher education for all. Public institutions are also partially funded by the government through their budgets. Public colleges and universities have in-state and out-of-state tuition differences and are vulnerable to political grandstanding which often creates budgetary issues (like increases in tuition). You might think of big name schools with tens of thousands of students when you think of public institutions, but every state also has much smaller, intimate public colleges and universities too.

For-Profit

For-profit schools are run by a corporation to generate a profit and often look to educate non-traditional students who need flexibility in scheduling and degree programs. Often, for-profit schools offer credit waivers for time spent in your career field or do not have entrance requirements for prospective students. For-profits have been known to aggressively seek out and recruit military members and their spouses and many are under current federal investigation for fraud or illegal practices.

Being Your Own Best Advocate

As a military spouse, you know how to advocate on behalf of your family and spouse. Advocating for yourself is no different. From the first Google searches for your degree program until you get that diploma in your hands, you'll want to make smart choices and do your research.

Accreditation

Pay particular attention to accreditation, especially if you're looking at attending a religious or for-profit institution. Accreditation is simply the process that schools go through to get a stamp of approval from educational organizations that ensure schools are keeping standards and are doing what they say they'll do—educate students. This process happens every few years, and while it's not common, it is possible for schools to lose their accreditation or never earn it at all. If your school is not accredited, it basically means that your degree is less viable because the education you received was not as rigorous. You'll want to make sure that your school is regionally accredited if you're attending an academic program. This will make it easier to transfer credits, go to grad school, or have a respectable diploma that will interest employers.

US Department of Veterans Affairs

If you're using the GI Bill, you'll want to bookmark the VA's website (http://www.benefits.va.gov/gibill/) where you can find the nitty, gritty details, a college search of VA-approved institutions, and a lot of other information helpful for attending college on governmental benefits.

Lodge a Complaint

With the influx of educational funds going to military members and their dependents, there has been an uptick in misleading programs and promises made to the military community by certain schools and programs. Make sure that you document everything and check it against the rules for your educational benefits. If you think the school you're attending is taking advantage of you or is misleading you, you can file a complaint and report the institution using these instructions: http://www.militaryonesource.mil/voluntary-education/complaint.

Ready to take the plunge? It's an exciting time for you! With a little bit of research and a lot of sticktoitiveness, you'll be on your way to academic and career success in no time!

7

Military Proofing Your Career

J.D.

When you marry a military member, you know you're in for an adventure of PCS moves, deployments, separations, and more. For those career-minded military spouses, this can be a little nerve-wracking when thinking about your career path. You think to yourself, *I've worked hard for my education, so the reward should be a decent career*. Well, when you become a military spouse, that dream job gets a little fuzzy. As a military spouse with a (I think) decent career in marketing, I can say this to you from experience: all is not lost. There are a few things you can do to military-proof your career.

Building Your Resume

Writing a strong resume is your first task in your job hunt. Decide whether you want to have a skills-based or chronological resume. The former works if you don't have a lot of experience. The latter is the most common resume. Create a great cover letter that is tailored for each job you want to apply for. Use action words and highlight how you can make the company better. Proofread. Proofread. Proofread.

Tips for Your Resume

- Use power action verbs over more passive terms
    - i.e. "managed" over "coordinated", "strategized" over "brainstormed"

- Use hard numbers when you can
    - i.e. Family Readiness Group leader for over 200 Sailors and their families, raised $3000 in unit fundraising activities over one year

- No need for the objective statements
    - Objective statements only make sense when you're in the middle of a huge career change and need to explain why

your experience doesn't match up with the job you are applying for.

- Summary statement/profile

    o Instead of objectives, you can try incorporating a short profile or summary statement about yourself. Consider it your elevator pitch. It should contain no more than 2-3 sentences.

- Avoid clichés

    o Common clichés include: detail-oriented, team player, hard-worker

- Design for quick reading

    o Most hiring managers will skim the resume first to see if anything jumps out about the candidate. Make sure you have the right headings bolded or italicized for impact.

- Format in PDF

    o Not all computers or operating systems are made equal. If the instruction requires you to send an electronic version, save your resume as a PDF and send (see Appendix A for a printable sample resume and a printable resume building worksheet).

Federal Jobs for Military Spouses

When you arrive at a new duty station, try to use military spouse preference to your benefit. Make sure your federal resume is optimized for the job announcement. Create job alerts for the fields you want on usajobs.gov.

In essence, a Federal resume is unlike any common civilian resume in every shape or form. The Military Spouse Preference (MSP) program maintains eligibility requirements.

Eligibility for MSP (You Must Meet All of These):

- You are the spouse of an active duty military member of the armed forces, including the US Coast Guard, relocating because of permanent change of station orders.

- Marriage to your sponsoring service member must take place *prior* to relocating to the new duty station area.

- You are in the eligibility period beginning 30 days prior to your sponsor's report date at the new duty station.

- The position for which you are applying is in the same commuting area as your sponsor's new duty station.

- MSP will be granted if the applicant is rated among the "best qualified" group.

Applying for MSP

- Now you must register for MSP. Apply for Program "S," the Priority Placement Program for military spouses. This is the only way you can exercise your military spouse preference for an Appropriated Funds (GS) position (within the Continental United States (CONUS)).

- You can apply for the program through your local Civilian Personnel Office (CPO).

- You need to provide certain documentation, which includes a copy of your sponsor's PCS orders, a copy of an SF-50 (if you have prior federal employment experience) or your DD214 (if you are a former service member), a copy of your most recent performance appraisal (if you are a current or former federal employee), and other documentation, such as college transcripts or licenses, as required for the position.

- MSP can be applied for non-appropriated funds vacancies (NF 3 and under). Nonappropriated Funds (NAF) jobs are typically the jobs at the commissary or Family and Morale, Welfare and Recreation Command (MWR) or exchange.

- To use MSP for NAF jobs, you will need a copy of your sponsor's PCS orders. Attach this to your application when you return it to the NAF human resources office (HRO) and a request for MSP.

  In some cases, the hiring office may have a form you can fill out to request MSP. However, you may want to have your own written statement requesting MSP when you go to the NAF HRO.

- Military spouse preference expires two years after the check-in date on your spouse's orders. Some human resources managers pay no mind to it, some do. Try anyway.

Applying for Federal Employment

- Create an account with usajobs.gov.

- Enter the contents of your resume into their resume builder.

- Pull relevant keywords from the job announcement to include in your resume.

- Attach all necessary documents.

- You can have several resumes saved on usajobs.gov to apply for different positions.

- Sign up for email alerts so you don't miss a job announcement (some can open and close in a matter of a few days).

From personal experience as a prior Federal government employee, the process can take months and is easily very frustrating. Be patient and keep optimizing your resume.

Defense Contracting Jobs

On the other side of the coin is defense contract work. From personal experience, defense contractors don't view my "military spousehood" (Not a word? It is now.) negatively. They, more often times than not, view it as a strength because I am familiar with the client base and military culture.

I have experience both as a federal government employee for the Department of Defense and as a defense contractor employee. Luckily, the defense contractor employee application process is a heck of a lot easier. For the most part, these jobs are found on common job search engines. You apply to them as you would a "regular" job. There are certain websites dedicated to defense contracting jobs; look for "clearance jobs" or "defense contractor jobs".

Other Jobs for Military Spouses

Consider a Home Business

It is usually more flexible to your schedule. You are in charge of making your own money. Check with installation regulations first if you live in base housing, since you may need approval for your home business.

Think About Virtual Work

These opportunities include virtual assistance, IT work, graphic design, database management, call center services, and more. Just watch out for work-at-home scams. Be suspicious of anyone who asks for money up-front.

Broaden Your Scope

If you don't know what you want your career to be, focus on what you want to accomplish. For example, if you want to help people, think about teaching, health care, or administrative work. If you want to educate others, look into training or human resources. If you want to work with money, look into banking, insurance, or accounting.

Job Hunting Tips for Military Spouses

Update Your Resume

Do this for civilian and federal jobs. Add any and all relevant and new skills or accomplishments. This includes your LinkedIn profile (https://www.linkedin.com/uas/login). If you don't have one, definitely get one. It's like starting up any other social media account but this one is meant to be very professional.

Create a Job Hunting Email

I created an entirely new email address when I started the job process. It was easier to keep track of applications, status updates, job alerts, etc. Make sure it is still sounds professional (i.e. doejane.15@gmail.com).

Contact Your New Installation's Employment Assistance Program

Each service has different names for these programs, but contact information should be through your installation's Family Support Center. Email or call them about employment opportunities in your new area, resume check, or other job counseling.

Attend a Job Fair on Your Installation

These are great sources of information. Be dressed appropriately and bring resumes and portfolios. Check out Hiring Our Heroes and other military-associated non-profits that serve the military community.

Volunteer

This can be a great way to gain valuable skills and fill that gap on your resume. It may even lead to a paid position.

Sign Up with a Temp Agency

A temp agency can be a great segue into your career. It fills the resume gap, you make money, and you can also network with whomever you temporarily work and come away with a possible permanent position.

Be Flexible

You may not find a job in the same industry or field as your previous job, but you may still be able to use many of the same skills while gaining valuable new ones for the future.

Never Stop Looking

Even if you already have a job, the best time to find a job is when you already have one.

Keep Your Social Media Clean

As a military spouse, you should already have your social media accounts private. Perhaps you can just clean it up a bit because potential employers have been known to look for your accounts without your knowledge.

The job market can be shaky for normal people; military spouses have it that much harder. But it can be done. Focus on your dream and plan how you want to make it happen. Be flexible but always keep your focus. Network and use all of the resources that are available to you. You, as a military spouse, deserve a career too. It's up to you to make that happen.

8

Building a Strong Support Network

Jo

I am definitely not the quickest at making friends. I've never been a popular person. I don't go out much. But I do like having friends. I'm not a hermit. And being a military spouse is a little challenging for me on that end— I'll admit it.

For many spouses, it's tough leaving your friends and family and moving away. And then moving away again. And again. It's easy to wonder what the point is. After all, why should you bend over backwards to make friends every two or three years when you'll just leave them and be at square one? It's an easy defense mechanism to deploy.

But friends really make military life sweeter. And it's worth reaching out and trying to connect with the community.

Making Friends

There are all kinds of weird social rules that military spouses think they need to follow. Yes, you can be friends with an officer's spouse if you're an enlisted spouse (or vice versa). Yes, you can be friends with members of your spouse's command. Yes, you can go make friends in the wider community. You're not a leper or a pariah. You don't need to be in quarantine on base. The military doesn't dictate who you talk to and hang out with...unless you want it to.

Quick Tips for Making Friends

- Before you PCS, put an all-call out on Facebook or contact friends in your circle. Ask about possible connections for your next base. You'll be surprised how small the world is and how quickly you'll be able to find people at your next station before the move.

- Keep an open mind. Military spouses come in all shapes, colors, sizes, genders and religions. Maybe you've never had someone Muslim or Jewish as a friend before. Maybe you're a little nervous about how to approach the dual military lesbian couple next door. Or you're worried that your age might make a difference to the spouse who is anticipating her service member's retirement. If you write people off out of hand, you'll never have the chance to grow an amazing friendship with someone different than you.

- While we're at it—forget about the officer-enlisted divide. Maybe our service members can't hang out, but we can. There's absolutely no reason (social, military, or otherwise) that stops spouses of different ranks, Military Occupational Specialties (MOS), or any other division in the military from getting together.

- Okay, and one more thing: forget about the branch warfare. I know it exists (no matter how much we say it doesn't) because I've experienced it first-hand. At a networking event, the person I was talking to found out that we're a Navy family and turned around and walked away. Not cool. And really such a waste—because I'm a totally awesome person. (Just kidding. But really.) How many people did she walk away from simply because they didn't fit her specifications? We're all in this together, regardless of the branch our spouses serve in. It doesn't change the kind of person you are—how funny, sweet, or smart you are. Case in point: my closest friend at our current station is an Army wife. She rocks. Now, go make some cross-branch friends.

- Junk the Mommy-Not-Mommy divide. This seems to be something that plagues people in the civilian world, but it seems very acute in the military one. Truth bomb: Having or not having a child does not make you a better or worse person. It just makes you person with (or without) a child. Sadly, many times, mothers and non-mothers don't feel that they're welcome in the other group's lives. There are so many other things that spouses can connect with each other on—give the other group the benefit of the doubt (and widen your potential friend pool).

Keeping in Touch with Friends and Family

When I was a (very) young military spouse, I met many other spouses who had less-than-great relationships with their families. They saw military life as a way to escape dysfunction and frustration and keep a healthy distance between themselves and their estranged families.

But that wasn't me. And I couldn't relate to it. My family is near and dear to my heart. One of the hardest things about being a military spouse is living away from them. For many military families being away is a painful sacrifice made harder by frequent PCSing that always leaves friends behind.

Thanks to the wonderful ubiquity of technology, saying goodbye doesn't have to be goodbye forever. Or even for a few minutes.

Facebook

It probably goes without saying: Facebook is now the military spouse's address book. It's how we keep in touch, grow our networks and social circles, and stay up-to-date with goings on. Maintaining your Facebook and connecting to people that you know and trust is a fantastic morale-booster and way to save time—you can share your family's adventures with just one click of a button.

Instagram

If you feel a little squeamish about Instagram (especially if you have children), set your Instagram to private. Like Facebook, it's a streamlined way to share your daily lives with your friends and family who may want a glimpse of your life in Okinawa, Japan or your kids growing up in Twentynine Palms, California.

Viber

Like iMessage on iPhones, Viber is a free way to text and voice and video call others who also have the app downloaded. You just need to be connected to Wi-Fi. It's the best way I kept up with my sister who was abroad for a year—without spending a single cent on long distance calls.

Skype/Google Hangout

Video chatting. If you're not doing it, you should be— especially if you're really homesick. It's wonderful to be able to see your mom try to figure out whether or not the camera's on.

Vacation

Use vacation time to visit family and friends if you're able...or invite them to your neck of the woods! If you have a guest room available for visitors so a trip to Japan or Italy or California isn't so costly for them, so much the better!

When it comes to creating a circle of support and keeping in touch with family and friends, technology makes it easier than ever to stay in contact. If you're willing to reach out, you can. It's just a matter of doing it.

9

Becoming a Good Military Spouse

Lauren

You may wonder what exactly makes a good military spouse. As you meet countless military spouses over the years, there are several qualities that will stand out to you. When dealing with negativity in the military community, the good military spouses will impress you even more.

A few months back, I remember struggling during a deployment. My son and I were living in a foreign country trying to adjust and find our way around. I was angry that my husband was away during a time that I really needed him. It was hard not to feel angry at the military and the deployment for keeping our family apart so soon after our first outside the

Continental United States (OCONUS) PCS. My negative thoughts certainly weren't helping me any, and I decided it was time to phone a friend.

Any time you are part of a life where you move around a lot, experience frequent separations, and have a spouse with a demanding job, life feels challenging. You need support from other military spouses to carry you through, and honestly, other military spouses need your support as well.

The longer you travel the military life, the more you start to notice the good military spouses who stand out from the crowd. You see their countless great qualities and it's easy to see why they make wonderful friends to other spouses. These are the spouses you remain in contact long after you PCS from duty station to duty station.

When I first met her, I didn't realize what a great friend she would become. Months later, I was struggling and needed a pep talk. I picked up the phone and called her.

Signs of a Good Military Spouse

Be a Friend Others Want

Being a good military spouse doesn't mean you need to be front and center in the military spouse community at every function. It also doesn't mean you have to be friends with everyone. It simply means that you are a kind and generous friend to others.

Being a friend others want means making an effort to connect with a few spouses. Whether you are an introvert or extrovert, treat others well and reach out to spouses when they need it most.

Stay Away from Drama

In any walk of life, there is unnecessary drama. The military community is no exception. Great military spouses avoid it altogether. They stay away from gossip both online and in person.

Share Struggles

Good military spouses are far from perfect. Struggling is a normal part of military life and it's healthy to share those struggles with others. Venting to a close friend or family member is a positive thing.

Stay Positive

Military life is hard and challenging. Allowing less-than-desirable circumstances to get the best of you is far from ideal. Focus on positive things happening in your life, surround yourself with positive people, and use encouraging quotes or phrases to keep yourself going.

Prioritize Your Relationship

Military life puts a strain on even the healthiest relationships. Working hard to keep your relationship strong through honesty, communication, and quality time is well worth the effort.

Take Care of Yourself

As a military spouse, remember who you are as a person. Remember the hobbies you love and make special time for it. Remember to make time to do things outside of military life. Investing in yourself keeps you going in the long run through all the ups and downs of military life.

Seek Out Support

Even the best military spouses need support from others. Working hard to grow friendships, even if they are faraway friends, is worth it. Support gets you through the deployments, homecomings, PCS moves, and everyday obstacles.

Etiquette for Military Spouses

If you ever wonder how to greet someone your service member works with or how to dress for certain occasions in military life, this will help you learn the basics when it comes to military spouse etiquette.

Avoid Gym Clothes

Yeah, you can't go to Dunkin Donuts on base to grab a coffee in your gym clothes. (Not that I ever got yelled at for doing that.) Unfortunately, you can't go to the Commissary either or other on-base businesses if you are not dressed properly. At every military base, there is a dress code for the Commissary, Exchange, gas station, and other businesses. The dress code is an order that is normally posted near the front doors, explaining that civilian clothing must fit properly (not too tight, not too loose) and that patrons are prohibited from wearing pajamas, athletic shorts, swimsuits, and Spandex-type gym attire. Military dependents and their guests are a reflection of the military service member and it's important to respect military base rules. Rule of thumb: save your gym clothes for the gym and your jammie pants for your home.

Show Respect During the National Anthem

Being respectful while the National Anthem is played is an important way to show honor and respect. Gum chewing, talking, or smoking during the National Anthem is best avoided.

Refer to Your Spouse by Name

Whether you are at a formal or casual event or simply out and about on base, it is best to always refer to your service member by their first name or nickname. No need to refer to him or her by rank or as "Sergeant Smith" or "the Sergeant." That would be hilarious though.

When a Service Member Is in Uniform, Save the PDA

Unfortunately, as fabulously attractive as your service member looks in his or her uniform, PDA is prohibited. There are definitely situations when it is overlooked and very conservative hand-holding or a kiss may be okay. But for the most part, it's best to refrain in public. In private...that's a whole different story.

The Service Member's Uniform is for the Service Member

Thinking about using your service member's uniform for a funny Facebook post or sexy Halloween costume? Hold off. Wearing a service member's uniform as a civilian is considered disrespectful. As a general rule, only the service member should wear military uniforms. This includes formal wear, cammies, and gym clothes. Your spouse may get in trouble if photos of you or others are seen wearing their uniform.

Some spouses have had a photoshoot while wearing a service member's uniform. This unfortunately is a bad idea and should be avoided.

Walk on the Left Side When He or She is in Uniform

This leaves the right side available for your partner to salute if needed, and is just good practice overall. This doesn't mean you can never be near his or her right side, it simply means if you are walking closely or linking arms while he or she is in uniform, he or she will likely need to salute with the right arm. This may also mean carrying something for your partner in order to keep his or her right arm available.

Stop for Colors and the Raising/Retiring of the Flag

If you hear colors or see the raising or retiring of the flag, politely stop and face the flag with your hand over your heart. This includes if you are driving in your vehicle.

Avoid Conversations About Politics, Sex, and Religion at Special Events

This is just a good rule in military life and everywhere else. Avoiding the use of foul language while at special events is also a good rule of etiquette.

Know the "No Walk and Talk Rule"

Service members are discouraged from walking, talking, or driving while on a cell phone or walking and eating or drinking while in uniform. Eating in the car is considered okay at some installations.

RSVP and Write Thank You Notes

Responding to an invitation is both kind and polite and it's an easy gesture to do. Thank you notes are a bit of a dying art. A simple handwritten thank you note sent to another community member goes a long way and it only takes a few minutes' time.

Recognize ranks and Address Them Properly

There are a lot of variations between the different branches, so my best advice is simply to ask your service member if there are any he or she would like you to know. You may wonder why you would really need to know this information. The answer is simple:

Addressing a higher-ranking official in the military is a sign of respect that is well deserved. If you are interacting with a higher-ranking official, plan to formally address them by rank and last name until the individual asks you to do otherwise.

For example:

Official: "Hi, I'm Major Smith."

You: "It's great to meet you, Major Smith."

Official: "You know what? Call me John."

Once given permission to call him or her by name, it is acceptable to casually use their first name.

If you ever find yourself in a situation and you aren't sure about proper etiquette, simply smile and be polite and kind. Those things go a long way and there is no need to wrack your brain over rules and regulations.

Dealing with Negativity in the Community

The majority of the time, most military spouses maintain a positive outlook on military life. It provides families with blessings and opportunities. It helps spouses grow and become strong, independent people. It's allows military spouses to travel the world and meet amazing people.

There is another side to the military spouse community where military spouses bash other military spouses. This is known as military spouse shaming, and it is the dark side of military life. These are situations when military spouses, members of the military, or veterans tear down spouses who are sharing their weakest moments and most vulnerable struggles. It is disheartening to see.

When you witness negativity in the military spouse community there are things you can do to unite and create a more positive, supportive, and welcoming community. Because we are all in this together.

Dealing with Dependa

If you don't already know, you may wonder what exactly is a dependa or dependapotomus?

According to Urban Dictionary, it is "traditionally a service-member's dependent who is a 'stay-at-home mom' that doesn't do a damn thing all day besides sitting on the couch looking remarkably similar to jabba the hut [sic] leaching off of military benefits and eating anything that gets too close."

Being a military spouse does not mean that you are invincible. It doesn't mean that you aren't allowed to feel sad, upset, or angry about military life. And it certainly doesn't mean that you are a dependent woman, who eats bonbons all day long just because you struggle from time to time.

Military spouses are independent, loyal, educated, strong, smart, and savvy people, and they still struggle just like everyone else. Admitting to struggling is a brave and courageous thing to do. Most aren't willing to do so. When you see a fellow military spouse struggling, encourage, help, and guide him or her.

Dealing with the Labels

One of the most challenging parts about the military community is that you are supposed to sit down, shut up, and suck it up. Stop complaining. Stop whining. A minority of spouses cried wolf one too many times, and people are sick of the complaining.

However, the majority of spouses share their struggles in an effort to cope and work through real issues in a healthy and constructive way. We all know that one of the unhealthiest things that you can is to bury your problems and never talk about them.

It's okay to say things are hard. It's okay to say that you are struggling and to talk it out. It isn't taboo to share that you are an imperfect military spouse who isn't "just fine." Many spouses with the strongest marriages still struggle.

Dealing with the WESPAC Widow

What is exactly a WESPAC widow?

According to Urban Dictionary, it is "a US Navy wife who f*@^s [sic] around with other men while her man is out on deployment. Named for the West Pacific, or WestPac cruise, which is a common and lengthy deployment for West Coast sailors."

It's unfortunate that a few military spouses have ruined it for everyone. Many other military spouses wouldn't dream of ever cheating on their service member, let alone during a deployment.

This label is always used against women. There are service members who cheat on their spouses while they're on deployment. Women take the heat for the same behavior and are hated, but there are guys who do this garbage too, and there doesn't seem to be the same level of hate or vitriol for them.

It's important to choose our words wisely. Just because a spouse is sharing her struggles does not mean she is an unfaithful wife.

94

Phoning that Friend

Back to that night when I picked up the phone to call a friend: she was there. She answered. She listened. I felt so much better after that phone call, and it helped me realize that military life wasn't so bad after all. Being friends with a great military spouse encouraged me to become a better spouse myself. It helped me learn what being a good military spouse is about: doing a few little things to help others when they need it most, knowing a few etiquette basics, and staying away from negativity in the community.

10

When Children are Present

J.D.

If you decide to add or currently have children in your military family, you know that there's a list of other considerations you have to be aware of when it comes to military life for the kids. From PCSing to deployments to hectic schedules, there are several important ways to help your military kids thrive.

Pregnancy and Childbirth

Expectant parents have a lot of things on their mind before the arrival of their little one. For pregnant military spouses who are not active duty, there are important items to know and remember before delivery. There are also some benefits that military families should know about when they find out they are expecting.

Healthcare Coverage

As of 2015, TRICARE covers all medically necessary maternity care—from the first obstetric visit until six weeks after delivery. Depending on your enrollment status (Prime, Standard or Extra), some out-of-pocket costs are possible. As of August 1, 2015 TRICARE approved coverage for breastfeeding pumps and supplies. Consult your regional TRICARE office (http://tricare.mil/ContactUs/CallUs.aspx) for more information.

Deployment

If your partner is deployed, there are some options for open communication when it comes time for the delivery. Notify your FRG leader or Ombudsman about your pregnancy and anticipated due date. They are the first point of contact to your deployed service member when you go into labor. As a back-up plan, find out what information the Red Cross needs in order to contact your service member. If you are planning to deliver in a military hospital, contact customer service at the hospital for rules on video chats.

Classes

Each military installation may offer childbirth and parenting classes at little to no cost for expectant parents. Subjects can range from baby budgeting to newborn care. Depending on the budget and installation, you may receive a baby goody bag once the class is completed. If you're going to an obstetrician on base, inquire about classes during your first appointment.

Paternity Leave

Married service members who are new dads can now take 10 days of non-chargeable leave time. (An active duty mother can take up to six weeks, with sailors and Marines eligible for 18 weeks throughout the first year of the baby's life.) However, each branch has different rules and policies about the authorized window of taking paternity leave. To be eligible for paternity leave for any military branch, the service member must be active duty and married.

Solo-Parenting

You can easily get overwhelmed with the added responsibilities and stress of parenting when your spouse deploys. While the situation is temporary, you still must make adjustments to your emotional, mental, and practical day-to-day feelings and tasks.

When you know your spouse is about to deploy, you can prepare in advance to help make the transition easier. If you try to anticipate what might happen and discuss some of the issues you may face, deployment for the whole family goes a lot more smoothly. Consider the following when your military family is preparing for deployment:

Legal

First things first: ensure that your partner completes or updates the power of attorney (POA), wills, and family care plan before deploying. You will need these documents to act on his or her behalf. Make an appointment and have all of the necessary applications and corresponding documents ready beforehand (the base legal website or point of contact can tell you exactly what you need). If there is no planned a legal assistance preparation day via the command, contact Base Legal yourself. Have durable POA (in addition to a general POA) and legal guardianship set up for your kids in the event that something happens to both parents. The family care plan is a safeguard for your family, helping you and your service member generate a step-by-step childcare plan in the event of an emergency.

Emergency

Have contacts ready for any situation, from medical to car trouble to financial help. Each installation can provide you with a list of resources that may be available. Include the FRG leader or Ombudsman's contact information. If they are old enough, make sure your children can access and use this list.

Finances

Set up a joint bank account if you haven't already done so. Pay during deployment can fluctuate, depending on the environment. You can also get access to your spouse's Leave and Earnings Statement (LES) to make sure things are accurate. If there are issues with your joint account during separations, check with your financial institution to learn if you require a special POA to take action. (See Chapter 5 for more information about keeping your finances in order.)

Communication

Getting in touch with your spouse may not always be possible or consistent. If your children are old enough to understand that, explain it to them. Record videos or audio before the deployment to use while your service member is away. Children are often comforted by the sounds of their deployed parent's voice.

Child Care

Even if you don't have children in the military child care system, ask to see if they offer drop-in services for those times when you need a few hours to yourself. You must register your kids to be able to use this benefit. It also helps to have a few reliable babysitters on call—just in case. Look into childcare services offered through the USO, your child's school, and Military OneSource: http://www.militaryonesource.mil/family-and-relationships/child-care-and-youth-programs.

Helping Kids Cope with Deployment

When a parent deploys, family roles may change. New routines are established and new sources of support, such as relatives, friends, playgroups, and community gatherings are discovered. The following tips can help your children adjust to this transition:

Take Care of You

You first must take care of yourself and manage your own feelings about the separation. Talk to a friend or confidant to help you gain emotional balance. Keep open lines of communication with your spouse, as much as the circumstances of deployment will allow. This will put you in a more positive position to support your kids during a challenging time.

Communicate

Kids need to feel comfortable that they can ask questions and openly discuss their thoughts and feelings. Talk to your children often and honestly to help them work through their emotions and reactions. Adjust what you say about the deployed parent depending on the child's age and level of understanding.

Offer reassuring phrases that are not based on your service member returning home on a specific date. For example, "No matter what, Mom and Dad love you. We'll do everything we can to keep you safe." Or, "We are a family no matter if we are together or apart."

Connect

Keep in touch as much as possible with the deployed parent with emails, texts, phone calls, care packages, and letters.

Allow kids to feel connected to their deployed parent by writing a letter or drawing him or her a picture each day. You can also allow kids to take a picture for their mom or dad each day during the deployment. When the deployment is over, you can make a photo book to give your service member at homecoming.

You can also encourage your service member to leave something behind for each child. This could be an unwashed shirt for each child that they sleep in each night.

Help Your Child Navigate Emotions

Kids often do not understand what or why they are feeling something inside. If your child is angry, anxious, frustrated, or sad help them name the feeling. You can say, "You seem really angry right now about missing your mom or dad." Anything to help them label the what and why of emotions helps children cope.

If your child is old enough, encourage him or her to draw a picture of what your family looks like right now and tell you what he feels about the situation. This is a positive way to discover hidden emotions.

Another way to get kids talking and share feelings is to use an activity as a buffer. This could be anything—a board game, walking on a trail, doing a craft, or something else that they enjoy. Kids are more likely to open up and share stories while doing something to keep their hands busy.

You may feel like a broken record talking about feelings with your kids over and over again. This is one way children process stressful events—through repetition. If you feel like your child is asking the same questions over and over, stay patient. This is a sign of very healthy coping during difficult circumstances.

Stick to Routines

Family life shouldn't be "on hold" until the deployed parent comes home. Children find comfort in routines and feel more secure if important family rituals remain unchanged (i.e. bedtimes, mealtimes, game night)

Maintain Discipline and Firm Limits

Your kids may test your rules and routines. Make sure they know that the regular household rules, like homework and chores, will not change during deployment. Maintain a clear and consistent set of consequences and rewards.

Stay Involved in Your Child's Education

Let teachers and educators know your family has a deployed parent and that your children may be facing extra stress. Ask them to look out for any signs of distress or trouble. Even if your school issued a school-wide military survey, often the results are not shared with your child's teachers, and they may not know about your family's circumstances. Clear, consistent communication with your child's teacher will help him or her offer support to your child when he or she is away from you.

Ask for Help

If you are struggling with parenting during a deployment, you are not alone. Contact your primary doctor for a referral to seek help from a counselor or social worker in your community. Even a few short sessions with a counselor can provide you with effective tools to turn a challenging situation around.

There are many deployment groups that are just for children. Contact your FRG to see what is available via your military branch in the local area. Deployment support groups for military are often active in schools and the military's parent support program. In support groups, kids can learn tools to manage feelings and connect with other children in the same situation.

Best Toys and Resources for Military Kids During Deployment

Daddy Dolls

This organization offers you the opportunity to purchase a doll with a deployed service member's photo printed on it. Daddy dolls provide a comforting item from which children can gain strength in the midst of challenging situations.

Dog Tags for Kids

This organization sends dog tags to troops currently serving in harm's way so they can send them to their kids back home. The dog tags serve as a special memento for children to hang onto while awaiting the return of their parent.

Flat Daddies and Flat Mommies

Flat Daddies and Flat Mommies are life-size photos of deployed service members. They are provided to help children better cope with the separation they experience when a parent is away from home for long periods of time.

Kids Journals

A children's initiative created to offer resources to help children better navigate the unique challenges military families face, these journals offer a different way for kids to express themselves. Easily review, download, and print journals related to deployment, military moves, and the death of a loved one for free.

Brats: Our Journey Home

A documentary about growing up in the military. U.S. military BRATS share personal memories about their unique childhoods, including lessons learned from life on military bases around the world and struggling to fit into a typical American lifestyle, which is so different from their own. Note: This is for older kids.

Sesame Street Workshop

An outreach program to help military kids through deployments, combat-related injuries, and the death of a loved one. Videos, storybooks, and workbooks are available through this program to guide families through challenging transitions by showing how real families (and our favorite Sesame Street characters) cope with similar situations.

United Through Reading

A military program that aims to ease the stress of family separation during deployment, Deployed parents read children's books aloud via DVD for their child to watch at home.

Photo Puzzle

Take a picture of your child with your service member before deployment. Next, order a photo puzzle through an online photo company and allow your child to put the puzzle together each day.

Voice Recorded Books

Grab a few more off Amazon and record several books of Mom or Dad reading a story to the kids before deployment. During deployment, read the story each day with your kids.

Best Toys and Activities You Can Make at Home

Make a Tell Mom or Dad List

Allow your kids to keep a running list of things they really want to tell their deployed parent. Then have them share those things in a letter, on the phone, or via Skype each time they talk.

Deployed Parent Box

Keep a box of items in your home that reminds your kids of their deployed parent. Allow the kids to pick out the items pre-deployment and have them open the box each time they miss their parent.

Deployed Parent Games

Play a made-up family game where you earn a point each time you name something the deployed parent likes or does. An example would be basketball, where you earn a point by making a shot and saying something about Mom or Dad. The first person to 10 points wins.

Deployed Parent Puzzles

Use online puzzle makers to create a crossword or word search about Mom or Dad.

Deployed Parent Dance Party

Sing or dance to songs only Mom or Dad likes. Video record it and post it on a private YouTube account to share with Mom or Dad.

Deployed Parent Kisses Countdown Jar

The jar contains Hershey Kisses to equal the number of days remaining in the deployment. Each day your child gets a kiss from their deployed parent, and when none remain, Mom or Dad comes home. This is useful since most younger kids cannot understand the concept of weeks and months. If the homecoming date gets pushed back, simply add in a few more kisses.

Deployed Parent Command Center

Create a special space in your home that is designated for all things about the deployed parent. Fill it with pictures, recorded books, and memories of Mom or Dad. This offers a tangible place kids can seek out Mom or Dad even when he or she isn't home.

Make Deployed Parent Dollars

Create fake money with Mom or Dad's photo in the middle that your child can earn when the deployed parents hears about something positive the child did. This is a creative way to offer kids an incentive for staying positive.

Do a Homecoming Project

Choose a homecoming project to do as a family. This could be taking a picture each day and then making a picture book using an online photo website to give to mom or dad at homecoming. This could also be sending out blanket squares to extended family to create welcome back messages. Have family members return the blanket squares and sew together to create a homecoming quilt.

Helping children cope during deployment is filled with ups and downs. Children of all ages may feel less secure because of a change in family structure during deployment. Please know that each military child is unique and responds differently to parenting strategies during a deployment. What works well for one family may be entirely different for another family. Be patient, keep the communication lines open, and seek out creative ways to connect with the deployed parent.

11
Ready to PCS?
J.D.

Frequent moves are a staple of military life. On the one hand, it allows you to explore different parts of the world we might not have otherwise. On the other hand, it can be stressful to uproot your life every few years. While some may think that the responsibility falls on the service member, PCSing is a team effort. Your family may be moving across cities, states, and even countries. It's a long and detailed process but with the right preparation, it can definitely be manageable.

Things to Do Before Moving Day

Research Ahead

Find out all you can about your next duty station: where to live, where the best schools are, how the job market is doing, etc. The FRG leader or Ombudsman can help guide you. There are also many different military-associated groups on social media for you to follow and ask specific questions to. There are some for active duty, spouses, families, and more. Knowing where you want to live is a great jumping-off point.

Plan for Your Journey

Think about how soon you want to be there. The service member has a check-in date to his or her new command. The family will still have to think about how early they want to arrive in order to house hunt, move in, job hunt, and/or get the family settled. Do you plan to do it yourself (also known as a DITY move) or hire movers? Do you plan travel by plane or take a road trip? If you plan to live in military housing, contact the housing representative to determine eligibility and wait times. If you plan to buy a home, consider doing a scouting trip beforehand.

Get Measurements

If you already have a house waiting for you at your new duty station, be sure to find out inside measurements for your new home. These measurements will help guide you on what to bring with you and what to leave behind.

Purge Before Packing

Once you decide what you're taking, it's time to purge the rest. Categorize your household goods (HHG) into four piles: keep, sell, donate, and discard. In terms of the timelines, get rid of your "sell" items first by holding a garage sale or conducting private sales. Whatever you don't sell, move to the "donate" pile. Be sure to get a receipt if you donate to an organization (it could help during tax time). Finally, whatever you weren't able to donate, recycle or dispose of properly.

Take Photos and Videos

When you have your "keep" items selected, take lots of photos and videos. You'll want to do this especially for the high-value items. (Consider hand-carrying those that you would be devastated over if they were lost or broken.) For electronics, include pictures of any wires, cables, accessories, and the serial number. For anything that turns on, video it working with a timestamp to prove that it worked prior to the move. If you're hiring movers or doing a partial DITY move, you'll want these photos and videos on record just in case something happens to them. Make sure the inventory list that the movers fill out is accurate and legible.

Decide on Your PCS Budget (and Stick to It!)

The service member may receive a Dislocation Allowance (DLA) to help offset the expenses of relocating your household due to a PCS. DLA is intended to partially reimburse relocation expenses not otherwise reimbursed and probably will not reimburse *all* of your relocation expenses. Therefore, stick to a budget for cleaning expenses, food, and perhaps temporary lodging. If you are renting or are in military housing, you can ask the community manager for pre-inspection for move-out so you'll know how much to budget towards cleaning up your house.

Set Aside Your Documents

During this time, it helps to create a storage or organization system for your PCS move. Most people use a binder or folder to keep all documents in check. You will want multiple copies of your orders as well as a place to keep your personal documents (Social Security cards, certificates, titles, etc.) with you during your move. If you hire movers, make sure they do not pack that binder.

Moving Day

The big day is finally here: Moving Day. You've done the prep work, now it's time to start the move. Whether you are doing a DITY or having movers, there are some tips that can make moving a lot easier.

Wash the Linens

Wash all of your linens that have been piled up in the back of your linen closet. If it looks and smells dingy, throw it out. This include curtains, tablecloths, napkins, etc.

Use Ziploc Bags

These bags are great for packing and keeping similar things together like utensils, silverware, toys, or that giant box of pens. Also use them to keep tools and hardware attached to their furniture. Pro tip: use plastic wrap to wrap silverware drawers' contents. Fast and effective!

Keep All High-Value Items Together

Make sure you're there when the recorder is writing down everything. If you have the boxes for electronics, leave it out for them to pack (otherwise they might shift any damage blame on you). Please remember where they packed the remote controls.

Purchase Sample Sizes

Liquids and chemicals don't get packed. In the month or two before you leave, don't buy large quantities of liquid or chemical items. Try buying sample sizes to avoid waste.

Get a Really Big Purse or Extra Travel Bag

Don't fill it up all the way. There will be last minute items or things that weren't packed or that you picked up during the transition of moving. Throw these items into the big bag.

Schedule a Playdate

You are much more likely to have friends offer to keep your kids when you are moving out than when you are moving in. Not only should you say yes to any offers of help with your kids, but you should actively ask for help on moving days. People are willing.

Don't Pack Everything

For ones with kiddos, leave a few toys out to entertain the little ones when the movers arrive. They'll also need some entertainment when you travel. If you can, call a babysitter to watch the rugrats while the movers are there. If you have pets, reserve some food and treats for your fur-baby.

Pack a First Day Box

As in, the box you need on your first day at your new place. Include toilet paper, paper towels, a shower curtain, pillows, sheets, the internet router, a few plastic dishes to eat with, and more toys for the kids.

Label Boxes Yourself

I know the packers might label boxes. From my experience, they either write it really small, really messy, or not at all. When you're unpacking, it'll be chaotic trying to find an exact item if you don't know which box it is in.

Empty

As in, empty the trash, the dishwasher, the refrigerator, the washer, and the dryer for anything that may be left behind.

Quality Check

If you're renting at your new place, take photos before you move in. Document anything and everything that could possibly be wrong. Turn it into the housing office or your landlord if renting off base.

Open One Box at a Time

Once you open a box, empty it completely then break it down. *Then* you can move on to the next box. Otherwise you will have a bunch of half-open boxes, and nowhere to put things.

Adjusting to a New Duty Station

Once you arrive at a new duty station, it may take some time to adjust. Some duty stations are easy to love. Others require a little bit more effort.

Get Lost

Discovering your new duty station is all about allowing yourself to get lost. It's an amazing way to get out of your comfort zone, discover hidden treasures, and find your way around. I'm horrible with directions and I even find ways to misuse a GPS. The best way to find out where you're going is really just to get lost and find your way back home.

Plus, if you get lost and need to ask for directions to find your way home, it's a great way to introduce yourself to another local and meet a potential new friend.

Learn Where Things Are

Nothing will help you feel at home more than knowing where all your essentials are located. Likewise, knowing where all your go-to places are will help offer comfort and a sense of home.

Make Yourself the Friend Everyone Needs

Making new friends at your next duty station is essential to enjoying life. But wait! Making new friends is hard. So my best tip for making new friends is always to be the friend everyone needs.

There really is only one way to guarantee that you will have a friend who understands exactly what you're going through and will be there to offer up all the support in the world: you must be that great friend yourself.

Do Something That Makes You Uncomfortable

Staying home all day watching a How I Met Your Mother marathon and drinking too much coffee won't make you feel very at home in the long run.

Get out in your community and join a local group or even head to a local park or coffee shop. You never know what friendly people you will meet or fun discoveries you will make.

Find That One Place

Seek out and discover a local place to call your own hangout. It could be a restaurant you head to every Thursday night to play Bunco or it could be a coffee shop you visit every Saturday morning. Finding one local place to call your own can help you feel a part of your local community.

Pursue Your Interests

Attend meet-ups and get-togethers to meet new people. Pursue your interests socially. For example, if you're into fitness, take some exercise classes. If you're into cooking, check out the farmer's market.

Take a Picture Every Day

Yes. Take pictures. Lots of pictures. Creating memories of all the things you find from duty station to duty station will make you feel at home today and it will help you create fond memories to look back on years later.

With some time and positive thinking, any duty station can turn out to be a great one. Just keep an open mind.

12
Moving and Living Overseas
Lauren

Preparing for an OCONUS PCS takes a significant amount of busy work. Over a year ago, my husband and I prepared for our first big overseas move. The arduous process of compiling and completing all the necessary requirements for moving overseas was so tedious that we felt elated finally arrive at our new duty station.

Soon after, we settled into temporary lodging on base and eventually received an official offer for base housing. Looking back, there are so many things I wish I knew before moving overseas. More tips, hacks and consistent information can make the process less stressful and run smoother.

If you are preparing for an OCONUS PCS, here are a few things that will help military families navigate OCONUS PCS more efficiently:

Before You Have Official Orders

In order to make any major overseas moving preparation, you will need a copy of web orders first. If you anticipate an overseas assignment, however, you can prepare a few things in advance to help make life easier. This will also help you hit the ground running once you officially have orders in hand.

Here are a few things to keep in the back of your mind:

- Start to budget and plan financially for the PCS. No matter where you move, there are many out-of-pocket expenses before reimbursement.

- Organize important documents into one PCS file folder.

- Think about what to do with your vehicles. Learn if your host country will allow you to ship a vehicle. Usually you can only bring one, if shipping is even allowed. Decide if you want to ship, store, or sell your vehicles and carefully evaluate which option is the best financial decision for your family.

- Brainstorm what you want to carry in luggage, ship overseas, or store stateside. Just something to keep in the back of your mind before starting the process.

- Learn as much as possible about moving pets overseas (if applicable).

- Plan ahead for possible school options for your kids (if applicable).

Take a Class

The best way to obtain important information about your specific OCONUS PCS is to take a class on base. You may need to be proactive with finding information about classes available to you. If information is not readily available, ask your Family Readiness Officer (FRO) or FRG for guidance.

In the moving class, you will receive important information about moving to your host country, as well as important reference materials. Utilize your reference materials to help you throughout the overseas process. Moving overseas can feel very overwhelming, which makes it easy to forget the important tasks you need to complete. Rereading your reference materials several times can help you avoid missing anything.

Gather Important Paperwork

There is a large amount of paperwork required for an overseas move. You can start to gather some of the paperwork as soon as possible. This is not everything you will need, but maintaining copies of everything listed will ensure a smoother transition and minimize stress.

Must-have documents for an OCONUS PCS:

- PCS orders (original; make several copies)
- Overseas area clearance/dependent entry approval (original; make several copies)
- Family care plan
- Passports (one for each person traveling)
- Identification card for each person (if applicable)
- Current driver's licenses or permits
- Immunization records for service members and each family member traveling
- Medical and dental records
- Original birth certificates
- Naturalization paperwork (if applicable)

- Social security cards (including children)

- Marriage licenses and/or divorce decrees

- All education documentation (including kids' school transcripts)

- Deeds and titles to all real estate and other property

- Shipping and storage documents for your household goods

- Insurance policies

- Adoption papers (if applicable)

- Wills and power of attorney documents

- State and federal income tax returns

- Exceptional Family Member Program (EFMP) documents (if applicable)

Apply for No-Fee Government Passports

No-fee government passports enable you to travel **between the United States and your host country during your tour of duty**. If you plan to leave your host country to travel to a country **besides the United States** during your tour of duty for leave, vacations, or emergency family situations, you will need a personal passport for each family member.

Basically, it is best to have both types of passports—a no-fee government passport and a personal passport. Prepare and apply ahead of time for your government passport, which is usually handled by your branch's Travel Management Office (TMO). As long as you have web orders, you can start the government passport process. For your personal passport, apply through the Department of State (http://travel.state.gov/content/passports/english.html/).

Apply for a Sponsor

What is a sponsor? A sponsor is typically another service member who works in the same department as your spouse and is already established in your host country. During your OCONUS preparations and initial time in your host country, you will want a sponsor to guide you along the way. Your sponsor helps offer guidance during the overseas screening process, in addition to helping you get settled after your initial arrival. They will help you obtain cell phones, a car, lodging, and driver's license, and they will most likely show you around a bit. Moving to a foreign country with a sponsor will help you find your way, get settled, and minimize stress.

Apply for Area Clearance

Pick up the necessary paperwork to start the area clearance process. This is for **family members only**, and it is the process you complete to ensure you are medically suitable to move to the host country. Your service member will handle his medical clearance through military medical.

To start the area clearance process, pick up the paperwork at your local naval hospital or where you are directed. Next, make an appointment with your primary care provider to sign off on the medical paperwork. You will need a copy of your immunization record at your area clearance appointment. If you cannot find it, the doctor's office can draw blood to verify your required immunizations. After completing the medical paperwork for all family members, return it for review, and wait for instructions on the next step in the process.

Toss, Downsize, and Organize

The first thing you really need to know is your weight limit to gauge how many personal possessions you can bring to your host country. Think about what you really need and how often you really use items in your home. Consider donating unnecessary possessions to a thrift shop or community organization. If you own valuable items that you don't want to give away, consider listing them on a yard sale online or website such as Craigslist.

Next, think about what you will put in storage instead of moving it overseas. We took most of our essential and favorite pieces of furniture, storing pieces of furniture that we rarely used as well as most of our garage's contents. One thing you will absolutely want to take is your own mattresses and any piece of furniture that you truly love and use regularly (space allowing). 2-3 years is a long time, and after 6 months go by, you will start to wish you brought it along.

Leave behind irreplaceable valuables and family heirloom items. Examples include wedding albums, pictures, expensive art work, antiques, and anything else that you feel is priceless. Any time movers are in possession of your belongings, there is a chance the original item could be damaged or lost forever.

Pack Luggage Wisely

When preparing to pack your luggage, consider what you will need for the next several months. Typically you are allowed two bags per person, in addition to one carry-on and one personal item per person. You will look ridiculous carrying all this luggage, but once you arrive in your host country, it will save you the expense of purchasing many things you already own. Express shipments can take as long as 45 days and regular shipments can take up to three months. This is not a guarantee and in all likelihood, you will be without your possessions for quite some time. As the days and weeks elapse, you will feel grateful for all the possessions you brought in your luggage.

Here is a list of things you might consider packing:

- Set of bed sheets for each family member

- Set of towels

- Toys for kids (if applicable)

- Baby essentials (if applicable)

- Pillows for sleep

- Chargers and electronic devices (compatible with host country)

- All important documents

- Money (US and host country's currency)

- Fan for white noise

Determine the Best Option for Your Vehicle

Moving overseas puts you in an awkward predicament when selling a vehicle. If you can take your vehicles with you, by all means do so. If you are not allowed to bring them overseas, you maintain your vehicles well, and they are paid off, consider storing your vehicles.

Typically, you need your vehicle until very close to your move date, which is a less-than-ideal situation when it comes to negotiating a good sales price. Time isn't on your side and you are more likely to sell your vehicle for less than it is truly worth.

There is no perfect option for managing a vehicle during an OCONUS PCS. Evaluate your options and decide what is best for you.

Determine if Your Pets Can Come Along

If pets are a part of your family, be wary of the potential expenses involved with moving a pet overseas. There are very limited slots available for pets on the Patriot Express. If the government books you on a Patriot Express flight (http://www.eur.army.mil/PatriotExpress/) and there is no room for your pets, you still must take the flight.

This means you will need to find a way to get your pets overseas (if you choose to do so) and you will be responsible for paying all expenses. This can run anywhere from hundreds to thousands of dollars.

What to Pack in Each Shipment

When you move overseas there will be three shipments: express baggage, household goods, and temporary non-storage.

What do each of these mean?

Express baggage is a small shipment of household essentials to get you by until your larger household good shipment arrives. From your pack date, this typically takes about 6-8 weeks to arrive at your destination. Good things to pack in this shipment include:

- Kitchen items

- Clothes

- Bedding and pillows

- Toys (if applicable)

- Crib for baby (if applicable)

- Trash cans

- Shower curtains

- Everyday household items needed as soon as possible.

Household goods is your major shipment to your overseas host country. From your pack date this typically takes about three months to arrive at your destination. Good things to pack in this shipment include:

- Furniture

- Appliances (if applicable)

- Seasonal items

- Household decorations

Non-temporary storage is usually the last shipment to get packed from your home. This shipment contains everything you plan to store stateside while living overseas. Once you move back stateside, this shipment will be sent to your new home. Items to pack in this shipment include:

- Seasonal items that will not be used in your host country

- Furniture items too big for overseas housing

- High-value, sentimental, or irreplaceable family heirlooms.

- Anything unnecessary to take overseas.

How to Prepare Financially

When moving in the military, there are always associated expenses. Many are reimbursed; some are not. Preparing financially for an upcoming OCONUS PCS will minimize stress and help the process run smoother.

Here are a few expenses to prepare for during an OCONUS PCS move:

- **Temporary lodging.** You may need to cover this expensive upfront and the government will reimburse you at a later date.

- **Vehicle purchase.** If you anticipate a vehicle purchase, have cash set aside. You will also want money readily available to pay for registration, insurance, and any other vehicle expenses needed initially.

- **Replacement of household items.** Almost all moving companies will not move liquids or food to your next duty location. This means you will need to replace all your cleaning supplies, toiletries, and food once arriving in your host country.

- **Clothing.** Different duty stations often involve different climates. You may need to invest a

135

substantial amount of money changing your wardrobe.

- **Food.** Before, during, and immediately after a PCS move, you will consume significantly more convenience food and restaurant food. Prepare to have extra money set aside to cover this expense, while trying to eat home-cooked meals as much as possible.

- **Moving products.** You may need new or additional luggage to help you through this big move. You may also end up purchasing other moving products such as totes, bags, or other storage/organizational containers once arriving in country.

Please know that paying for temporary lodging and vehicles within the first month of arriving in your host country can up run thousands of dollars. Paying for two used vehicles and temporary lodging, plus moving products, food, and the replacement of household items cost our family around $6,000 when we moved overseas. Note: We used the money from the sale of a stateside vehicle to pay for our new vehicles once in our host country. Please check the reference materials provided for your specific host country to help you determine how much this may cost you.

Dealing with Culture Shock

There are many differences when moving to a brand new country that will overwhelm you at first. Many locals around your military base may know English; many may not. Learning new customs, experiencing language barriers, and living far from American faces are just a few things that make take some adjusting.

Take a Deep Breath

Everything new in life involves a period of adjustment. Take a deep breath and know that things will get better. Countless military families before you overcame the initial shock of living overseas and adjusted well over time. Reach out to your sponsor for help during the first few weeks and months in country.

It Takes Time

It's normal for you to feel out of sorts when moving overseas. From new to seasoned military families, everyone faces an adjustment period. If it takes longer than expected, that's okay. It's so normal. Really, it is.

Feel Encouraged

Regardless if you absolutely love living overseas or if you absolutely look forward to moving back to the US, every tour of duty is temporary. One day you will prepare to move to another duty station, look back on your time overseas, and appreciate the valuable adventure of a lifetime you experienced.

Preparing for OCONUS PCS involves a lot of work, but it truly is worth it in the end. After arriving in your host country, you will enjoy the adventures of a lifetime. Make the most of it, hang on, and enjoy the ride.

13

The New Rules of Social Media Engagement

Lauren

The world of technology dramatically changed over the past decade. It seems like everyone owns a smart phone and stays connected regularly through social media. I know I do! As a military family, you and your spouse must carefully decide what to share with others about your family's military affiliation, as well as what to share with others about your personal life.

What is OPSEC and PERSEC?

OPerations SECurity, or OPSEC, focuses on protecting unclassified information about military operations that can be used against service members or your family. It involves protecting information about where you are presently and where you plan to be in the future. Many times we share information with a loved one and think nothing of it. But it's important to think beyond that. What effect would that information have if it accidentally reached a harmful person somewhere else in the world?

PERSEC is short for PERsonal SECurity and it is used alongside OPSEC to protect the flow of information to non-essential people. PERSEC means protecting personal info about a person/soldier/civilian to prevent it from falling into the wrong hands.

The whole idea of OPSEC and PERSEC is a little confusing though, right? What can you safely share and what is best kept private? How do you make sure your family is safe from others who may use that operational or personal information to harm your family or service member?

Social Media Basics

There are few simple and easy ways to always keep yourself in the green light when dealing with OPESEC and PERSEC. This will keep you from feeling overwhelmed when you aren't really sure what you can and cannot do.

Change Your Settings to Private

Whether you are on Facebook, Twitter, Instagram, or another social media outlet, move your settings to private so that only the friends who you accept to your account can see your postings. If you are not able to do this, it is safe to assume that everything you post is public for anyone to see.

Accept Friend Requests Cautiously

Make sure you know and trust the individuals you add as friends on social media. Anyone can create an account to look like a friendly military spouse. Keep yourself safe and screen people carefully before accepting a friend request. Those individuals can see your entire profile and can copy, paste, and save any photos you share in your profile.

Don't Assume Facebook Groups Are Safe

There are a multitude of military community and military spouse social media groups online. Unfortunately, trolls lurk everywhere and can migrate into these groups without anyone noticing. If you are a part of a social media group, assume what you share will be public knowledge even if the group is secret or private. There is no way of knowing who was accepted into the group by the group administrator.

Choose Wisely What You Share

Be careful what you choose to share online with others. Even if your settings are private, it's important to remember that individuals viewing your profile can take your information and share it however they please. If you post a photo of your family, someone can still download the photo from a social media site or take a screenshot of it and upload it anywhere on the internet.

Don't Share Current and Future Events

Instead of sharing where you are at the current moment or your plans for future weeks and months, stick to sharing things that have already happened in your life.

Instead of: "My service member is leaving in a few days. I'm so bummed!"

Try: "We are enjoying our family time together."

Instead of: "My service member just got to Afghanistan. Only 7 more months of deployment"

Try: "We are keeping busy and staying positive around here lately."

It's perfectly fine to share life experiences that already happened. The goal is really to avoid screaming things like, "Hey, I'm right here at the moment. Come get me!" or "Here's where my service member is currently located."

It is also best to avoid sharing or talking about upcoming training missions, deployments, or homecomings. After the fact? Share a family picture if you'd like, but leading up to the deployment or training exercise, share only on a need-to-know basis via private communication with people who are safe. If you think about it, sharing that your service member is leaving basically tells the world that he or she is embarking on a mission and that you are home alone...and that is a scary thought.

For added protection, block out nametags and insignias which publicly declare your service member's name, job and rank. If you post a picture online, anyone could take a screenshot and inadvertently (or purposefully) share it with the wrong person.

Protect Your Children's Identities

One thing you may consider doing is giving your child a nickname when posting or sharing information online. Avoid using real names since people who know you already know your kids and their names.

Keeping Yourself Safe Beyond Social Media.

Disable the GPS on Your Phone

It's crazy how much your smart device tracks for you. Did you know that your smartphone might be tracking your every move without you even knowing it?

If you go to iPhone → Settings → Location Services → System Services → Frequent Locations, you will see that your iPhone has the ability to track your every move and put a time and date stamp on it too. Apple assures users that this information will be kept private, but what if someone hacks into your phone or it is lost or stolen? Someone would be able to find every place that you normally frequent.

Additionally, if you go to iPhone → Settings → Location Services, you will see all the apps that have access to your location. You can turn them off altogether or decide which ones you are okay with knowing your location. Most users want the maps application to use location services in order to offer directions and GPS services.

For Android users go to Settings → Location → Turn off.

Avoid Military-Affiliated Stickers

We all want to show our patriotism and serve as proud members of the military community, but our sense of security is different now. And when it comes down to it, I would rather be safe than sorry. Placing a bumper sticker or magnet on your vehicle that showcases a military affiliation makes you an easy target for dangerous people. They can follow your car to see where you live and the places you frequent. For now, it's best to remove the bumper stickers from the car as well as the stick families that showcase the exact number kids and pets you have.

Be Aware of Your Surroundings

No need to obsess or fear normal everyday activities, but keep your eyes peeled for unusual people or suspicious activity. Just know that someone may try to take advantage of you and your situation and it's best to be cautious. If something doesn't feel right, remove yourself from the situation, call someone you trust, and if needed, always feel comfortable getting the authorities involved.

Report, Report, Report.

If you are concerned about something, trust your gut and call your local military police. They take threats to military families very seriously and know best how to respond to suspicious activity. Even if you think it's nothing, what is the worst that can happen? You'll find out everything is safe and no harm is done. The authorities are here to help protect us and you should feel confident asking for help.

In our area, military community members often call military police for basic vandalism, suspicious people, kids in need of supervision, and so much more. These are all basic things that the military police receive calls for and they are happy to help.

OPSEC and PERSEC are part of everyday life in the military community. Often enough, using common sense will land you in a safe direction. Think carefully about what you post online and keep your eyes peeled during everyday activities. Taking a few actionable steps will protect both you and your family in the long run.

14

Conclusion

Lauren

It's hard to believe that seven years ago, I had just broken up with a doctor, and I was on one of those "I hate men" campaigns—having the time of my life with my newfound single status. It's even harder to believe that seven years ago I met my husband for the first time at a wedding in the Midwest. He had traveled from his duty station to see his childhood best friend marry my college best friend.

It was quite the wedding too. Over 300 guests from a small town came together in celebration of a happy and romantic young couple. I spent the majority of the night dancing and chatting with close friends.

And then I met him...

He was tall, dark, and handsome. So cliché, yet so true. We clicked instantly. He was active duty and I was a nurse working for the Veterans Administration. Our passion for veterans and patriotism brought common ground to the conversation. After chatting for a while, he asked me to dance and I answered with a resounding, "Nope!"

Still set on my man-hater rampage, I wasn't going to let him swoon me. Or so I thought. A bit later into the night and I conceded, allowing him to take my hand and walk me to the dance floor.

That was the beginning of our journey. It probably sounds more glamorous than it really was. At the end of the night, we parted ways without exchanging any contact information. He returned back to the East Coast; I returned back to everyday life as a single nurse living in the Midwest.

A few weeks later, he returned on pre-deployment leave and again our paths crossed. It really was special, but in typical military life fashion, it was also bittersweet. We hung out at a barbeque for one evening and that was the last time I saw him before he deployed. Thankfully we exchanged contact information that time around and over the course of seven months, we wrote email after email after email, spending our time growing a friendship.

As challenging as military life is sometimes, it also forces you to invest in each other in creative ways. When you really want to be with somebody, you find a way to be close to them even when you are thousands of miles apart.

Looking back now, my journey in military life feels surreal. I learned so much about myself in the most unexpected ways. Through deployments, homecomings, PCS moves, making new friends and so much more, I regularly appreciate all of the ups and downs. Each challenge and victory served great purpose: to build and nurture the foundation of my life as a military spouse.

You're here on this military life journey alongside us, and I know you have a story too. As a military spouse, you're filled with courage, resilience, and independence you never realized was possible. You work through all your own unique military life challenges and victories as best as you know how. All the big hurdles you overcome each and every day are what make you an amazing military spouse or significant other.

Whether you are a military spouse passionate about military life or struggling to find the hidden treasures in your journey, you are traveling an important road. You are the cornerstone of your military family. You are the person keeping your family woven tightly together on this military life journey. You often take the higher road despite frequent temptation to take the easy way out.

If you ever feel lost on your military life journey, you are not alone. Military life is hard. It's not the hardest or the worst, but it is hard. We are here with you. And if you ever feel a strange affinity for military life, likewise, you are not alone. J.D., Jo, and I are here right alongside you on this military life journey.

We hope you continue to stay connected with us!

15

Resources

Jo

Blogs

The Military Wife and Mom

Looking to parent with purpose, simplify motherhood and navigate the ups and downs of military life? Author of the rapidly growing parenting and military life blog, Lauren writes from the heart sharing no-nonsense tips, hacks, and ideas to help readers tackle life's everyday challenges.

Website: http://www.themilitarywifeandmom.com/

Facebook: https://www.facebook.com/themilitarywifeandmom

Twitter: https://twitter.com/mommilitarywife

Pinterest: https://www.pinterest.com/lauren9098/

Semi-Delicate Balance

J.D.'s lifestyle blog, Semi-Delicate Balance, features a little bit of everything. From motherhood to round-ups of inspirational quotes to advice for military spouses, you'll be able to find guidance and help for the journey.

Website: http://www.semidelicatebalance.com/

Facebook: https://www.facebook.com/SemiDelicateBalance

Twitter: https://twitter.com/SemiDelicateBal

Pinterest: https://www.pinterest.com/semidelicate/

Jo, My Gosh!

Begun while Jo was a military fiancé making care packages for deployment, Jo, My Gosh! has grown into a military lifestyle blog that focuses on relationships and military spouse empowerment.

Website: http://jomygosh.com/

Facebook: https://www.facebook.com/JoMyGosh

Twitter: https://twitter.com/JoMyGosh

Pinterest: https://www.pinterest.com/jomygosh1/

NextGen MilSpouse

NextGen MilSpouse is an online military lifestyle blog written by a variety of military spouses from all walks of life. It embraces diversity and looks to unify the military community through our commonalities rather than our differences.

http://nextgenmilspouse.com/

Resources

Army Wife Network

Offering a huge selection of Army-specific resources, Army Wife Network seeks to support military spouses, especially those who are affiliated with the army. AWN also has an online radio program and a Twitter chat that happen concurrently at 8 PM EST on Monday nights.

http://www.armywifenetwork.com/

Military Spouse

Available in digital and print editions, Military Spouse is a magazine written and edited exclusively by military spouses. Their print editions are available at the Exchange or by mail subscription.

http://militaryspouse.com/

USMC Life

USMC Life was founded by a military spouse who was trying to find information on different Marine bases... and just couldn't. USMC Life houses a repository of information, resources, and current events for USMC families.

http://usmclife.com/

SpouseBuzz

Part of Military.com, SpouseBuzz offers a military spouse perspective and community from the keyboards of other spouses. SpouseBuzz is most recognized for its timely opinions and informative articles about political and social issues and trends that affect military families.

http://spousebuzz.com/

Military One Click

Another website founded by a military spouse (sense a theme?), Military One Click provides career, education, savings, and veterans resources online and hosts in-person events throughout the year.

http://militaryoneclick.com/

Military OneSource

The Department of Defense program that provides resources to all members of the military family. Their 24-hour call center with master's-level consultants provide resources and referrals on everyday issues in military life from PCS to deployments to finances.

http://www.militaryonesource.mil/

Blue Star Families

From Blue Star Networks Live!, a program to empower and help milspouse and milfam entrepreneurs, to Blue Star Museums, a program offering free museum admission to military families during the summer, this organization constantly offers new resources and opportunities for military families.

http://bluestarfamilies.org/

National Military Family Association

To scholarships for milspouses to summer camps for children of Wounded Warriors, NMFA has programs, resources, and connections to help military families and support them throughout their military experience.

http://www.militaryfamily.org/

American Military Partner Association

AMPA offers support and information for LGBTQ military families and their allies by providing resources, a safe community, and political action.

https://ampa.org/

Education and Career

MyCAA

MyCAA, or My Career Advancement Account, is a governmental grant available to military spouses who are interested in pursuing portable careers. The grant is for up to $4,000 and does have some eligibility requirements and restrictions.

https://aiportal.acc.af.mil/mycaa/

Milspo Project

The Milspo Project is on a mission to connect military spouse entrepreneurs online and in person. The project offers an online community, yearly in-person conference, and 15 chapters around the country.

http://www.themilspoproject.com/

In Gear Career

Founded by military spouses for military spouses, In Gear Career offers both on- and off-line networking and educational experiences for career-driven spouses. If you don't live close to a chapter, you can always join In Gear's Facebook chapter which connects spouses from all over the globe.

http://ingearcareer.org/

Military Spouse JD Network

MSJDN exists to help military spouses who are legal professionals and deal with the obstacles of a very mobile military life. They lobby on behalf of those military spouses and also partner with other military organizations to bring projects like Homefront Rising to life.

http://www.msjdn.org/

Appendix A
Printables, Documents and Checklists

Deployment

Legal

- Write or update wills.

- Establish Power of Attorney.

- Consider a durable POA if you have children.

- Establish a plan of care if you have children.

- Make and keep multiple copies of documents (including birth certificates, POAs, and orders) on hand in case they are needed.

- Make sure that everyone has a government and civilian passport updated and ready in case of an emergency.

Financial

- Provide checking and savings account numbers.

- Inform bank or credit company if debit/credit cards will be used overseas for deployment.

- Set up joint accounts if necessary.

- Set up emergency savings accounts.

- Update beneficiaries.

- Set up a budget for home and deployment expenses

- Establish who will manage the budget and how withdrawals and expenses will be recorded.

- Create a plan of action for saving money during deployment.

- Research any financial opportunities and programs that may be available because of deployment.

- Have access to all financial information, accounts, and passwords.

- Know the dates of monthly loan payments and how to pay them.

- Have a plan in place for financial emergencies.

Healthcare

- Ensure family members are enrolled in TRICARE and information is updated and accurate.

- Ensure family members are enrolled in dental care and information is updated and accurate.

- Locate and record important medical information.

- List prescriptions, including dosages and frequencies.

- Gather vaccination and eye prescription records.

Auto

- Make and safely store spare keys for all vehicles.

- Sign up for roadside assistance.

- Prepare a roadside emergency kit.

- Create a schedule for oil changes and tune-ups.

- Record contact information of trusted mechanics.

Emergency Preparedness

- Create an emergency preparedness kit. Visit redcross.org for ideas.

- Establish and practice a home exit plan.

- Compile an emergency contact list

- Establish an off-site friend or relative to contact should you and your service member be unable to reach one another

- Have the FRG or Ombudsman's contact on hand (Follow their social media pages or get on their email list.)

- Be aware of possible emergencies that are common in your area (hurricanes, tornadoes, earthquakes, typhoons, etc.) and how to safely weather them— especially if you have not experienced them before.

PCS Moving

Be as complete as possible in preparing this list. There may be items that are unique to your situation that are not listed. This list is meant as a guide only.

8 Weeks Prior

- Create a PCS moving file (binders work well) to track expenses and hold important documents and receipts

- If you rent, notify your landlord or rental agent about the move. (Have your orders handy when you do so to avoid fees for breaking your lease.) If you live in housing, notify the housing office about your PCS orders.

- Call your realtor to begin the process of selling your home.

- Begin searching for a new home in your new location or contact the housing office at your new duty station.

- Notify your current employer of your impending move.

- Start the job hunt in your new duty station.

- Start looking at child care options and schools in the new area.

7 Weeks Prior

- Gather medical, dental, shot, school, veterinarian, and prescription records.

- Set up new doctors at your new duty station.

- Gather copies of legal and financial records.

- Call your insurance agent to make necessary changes to your policy.

- Contact gyms, organizations, and groups to cancel or transfer memberships.

6 Weeks Prior

- Plan how you will move (DITY or movers).

- Begin purging your home.

- Separate items into keep, sell, donate, or discard categories.

- Host a yard sale for unwanted items.

- Discontinue placing mail order purchases.

- Use items that can't be moved such as frozen foods, bleach, and aerosols.

- Discontinue buying large bulk items that can't travel.

- Check the Do Not Ship list for a complete list of items you can't move.

5 Weeks Prior

- File a change of address with the Postal Service.

- Prepare, update, and execute wills and power of attorney, or letter of authorization.

- Back-up computer files.

4 Weeks Prior

- Notify utility services of your move (both at your old and new locations).

- Make travel arrangements for your pets.

- Put copies of pet medical and immunization records in your moving file.

- Obtain copies of school records if you have children.

3 Weeks Prior

- Have your vehicles serviced.

- Notify debit and credit card companies of your move so your card is cleared for travel use.

- Plan stops along the way if you're traveling by car.

- Pick up the dry cleaning or any other items being repaired or stored.

2 Weeks Prior

- Set aside items to pack for travel.

- Confirm travel arrangements for pets and family.

- Plan meals for the last weeks to use up your food.

- Forward or place your mail on hold.

1 Week Prior

- Pack your travel bags.

- Inventory your items with a log and photos.

- Pack an essentials box to keep with you during the move.

- Drain gas and oil from lawn equipment, gas grills, heaters, etc.

- Drain water hoses and waterbeds.

- Empty and defrost the refrigerator for at least 24 hours before the move.

- Fill any prescriptions you will need during the move.

Moving Day

- Have plenty of water and snacks available to keep you or your movers energized.

- If you have a government-arranged move, obtain a copy of the Government Bill of Lading (GBL), the DD-619, and the Household Goods Inventory before the packers leave the residence.

- Check every room and closet one last time to make sure nothing is left behind.

- Leave a note with your new address so that future residents can forward stray mail.

- Clean up your space for the new occupants or hire a cleaning service.

Getting Married

- Obtain an original copy of your marriage certificate.

- Ask your spouse to enroll you in the Defense Enrollment Eligibility Reporting System (DEERS). This is how you receive the benefits. Your service member must enroll you. All service members and their dependents must be enrolled in DEERS to receive benefits. For the DEERS appointment, you will need a copy of your marriage license and the birth certificates or Social Security cards of all dependents, including children. Obtain a military identification card (dependent card) from the ID card facility. To receive benefits and access on military installations as a military spouse, you will need an identification card. All family members, including children ages 10 and older, will need their own ID cards.

- For the ID card appointment, you typically will need your marriage license, birth certificate, photo identification, and Department of Defense Form 1172 (application form) to apply for an ID card. Ask your spouse to list you as a beneficiary on his or her Serviceman's Group Life Insurance (SGLI) policy. Ask your spouse to update his or her record of emergency data sheet (DD Form 93). Memorize your spouse's Social Security number. You will need it for all sorts of paperwork and forms. Until you memorize the number, you can always get it from the ID card.

- Enroll in TRICARE and find a Primary Care Manager (PCM).

- Find housing. (This is optional.) Your service member may be entitled to additional pay depending on the branch of service, deployments, duty locations, whether or not you live on base, and other factors once you are married. You may want to live on base or in other housing.

To receive your free 22 printables included with this book, please visit the URL:

www.themilitarywifeandmom.com/modern-military-spouse-printables/

Password: MILITARY20

Appendix B

Abbreviations, Acronyms and Terms

Basic terms

Chit – A voucher requesting privileges or leave, usually signed by someone in authority.

Commanding Officer (CO): The officer in command of a military unit.

Commission – An official document issued by a government, awarding the rank of a military officer.

Department of Defense (DOD): The department of the U.S. federal government maintaining the U.S. military and national security.

Enlisted Member (EM): Any rank below that of a commissioned officer.

EAOS End of Obligated Service (EAOS): The date when service members are eligible for voluntary separation or retirement from the military.

ETS End of Time of Service (ETS): The date when service members set to discharge from the military.

Executive Officer (XO): The second officer in command of a military unit.

Personnel Support Detachment (PSD): A team assigned to protect the personal security of an individual or group.

Physical Training (PT): The physical training or exercise required of service members to meet military standards based on rank or military occupational specialty standard.

Uniform Code of Military Justice (UCMJ): The body of laws and legal procedures U.S. military members must follow.

Family Matters

Family Care Plan (FCP): A formal family care plan to help military families prepare for any period of separation.

Family Readiness Group (FRG): An organization of military members and family members who provide social and emotional support, outreach services, and information to families before, during, and between family separations, deployments, extended tours of temporary duty and field training exercises.

Family Readiness Officer (FRO): The person in charge of the Family Readiness Group.

Ombudsman: Similar to Family Readiness Officer, they can refer Navy families to various support agencies for assistance. The Ombudsman's major role is a bridge between the Command, its family members and the resources of the community.

Money Matters

Basic Allowance for Housing (BAH): An allowance to help compensate service members pay for housing expenses.

Basic Allowance for Sustenance (BAS): An allowance to help service members pay for meals.

Cost of Living Allowance (COLA): An allowance to help service members cover the cost of living in a specific geographical area.

Dislocation Allowance (DLE): An allowance intended to partially reimburse relocation expenses due to moving that are not otherwise reimbursed. DLA probably will not reimburse all of your relocation expenses.

Defense Finance and Accounting Service (DFAS): A service which provides finance and accounting support for service members.

Family Separation Allowance (FSA): An allowance to help service members with dependent family members cover expenses when the service member is required to be away from his or her permanent duty station for more than 30 continuous days in a TDY status and his/her dependents are not residing at or near the temporary station.

Leave and Earnings Statement (LES): A document given to service members each month, detailing their pay and leave.

Legal and Logistical Matters

CAC card: The modern identification card. It is also a smart card that is used with specialized card readers for automatic building access control systems, communications encryption, and computer access.

Defense Enrollment Eligibility Reporting System (DEERS): a computerized database of military sponsors, families and others worldwide who are offered TRICARE benefits.

Department of Veterans Affairs (VA): The department coordinating benefits for American veterans and their dependents. The benefits include compensation for disabilities, the management of veterans' hospitals, and various insurance programs.

Exceptional Family Member Program (EFMP): A program that works with military and civilian agencies to provide community support, housing, educational, medical, and personnel services worldwide to U.S. military families with special needs.

Military Treatment Facility (MTF): A facility that provides medical and / or eligible service members and families.

Power of Attorney (POA): A legal document that enables you to represent or act on another person's behalf in private affairs, business, or other legal matters.

Service Member's Group Life Insurance (SGLI): A program that provides low-cost term life insurance coverage to eligible service members.

Social Security Number (SSN): A nine-digit number issued to U.S. citizens, permanent residents, and temporary (working) residents.

Thrift Savings Plan (TSP): A federal government-sponsored retirement savings and investment plan for government employees.

TRICARE Military Health Care Program: A program that provides health benefits for military personnel, military retirees, and their dependents.

Uniform Service Identification Card (ID): An identification card issued by the United States Department of Defense to identify a person as a member of the Armed Forces or a member's dependent, such as a child or spouse. The card gives individuals access to military bases and provides proof of eligibility for TRICARE benefits.

Moving Matters

CONUS: Any military duty station within the Continental United States

Do It Yourself Move (DITY): A program where service members may move their personal property themselves, using rental equipment, their own vehicle, or by hiring their own commercial carrier. Military members can receive reimbursement up to 100% of the Government Constructive Cost (GCC), if they hire their own carrier, or an incentive payment of 95% of the GCC, if they move the property on their own.

Household Goods (HHG): All material possessions in your home.

OCONUS: Any military duty station outside Continental United States

Permanent Change of Assignment (PCA): The official reassignment of a service member within the same local area within a 50-mile region.

Permanent Change of Station (PCS): The official relocation of an active duty military service member – along with any family members living with her or him – to a different duty location.

Projected Rotation Date (PRD): The date a service member is expected to rotate to a new duty station.

Temporary Duty Assignment (TDA): A service member's travel assignment at a location other than the service member's permanent duty station. This type of travel is usually of relatively short duration, typically from two days to two months in length. Also known as TAD, TDT, TDY by various branches.

Temporary Living Expense (TLE): An allowance to help service members partially pay for lodging/meal expenses incurred while occupying temporary lodging as part of a CONUS PCS move.

Temporary Lodging Allowance (TLA): An allowance to help service members partially pay members for lodging/meal while occupying temporary lodging as part of a OCONUS PCS move

On Base Terms

Commissary: A grocery store on military bases.

BX Base Exchange (BX): A retail store on an Air Force base that sells goods to military personnel and their families or to authorized civilians

Marine Corps Exchange (MCX): A retail store on a Marine Corps base that sells goods to military personnel and their families or to authorized civilians

Naval Exchange (NEX): A retail store on a Naval base that sells goods to military personnel and their families or to authorized civilians

Post Exchange (PX): A retail store on an Army base that sells goods to military personnel and their families or to authorized civilians

United Service Organization (USO): A nonprofit organization that provides programs, services and live entertainment to U.S. service members and their families. There is often a USO office located on military bases as well as many off base locations, such as airports.

Vacation / Paid Time Off

Leave: Service members' paid vacation.

Sick call: Service members must see a military doctor when they don't feel well in order to stay home sick. Sick call hours are usually first thing in the morning, immediately following the breakfast meal.

Space-A: A way for service members, reservists, retirees, and military dependents to travel on military aircraft flights when excess capability allows.